Wheels for Sale

*The diary and memoirs of a
stroke survivor's husband.*

Mike Brewster

authorHOUSE®

This book is dedicated to our two wonderful daughters
Heather and Ailsa, their husbands Michael and Mark and
the grandchildren Jake, Callum, Henry, Zac and Joshua.

To our very close friends
Bill and Pat
Margaret and Keith
Polly and Ed
Barbara and Alan
John and Wendy
Rob and Cath
Mary and Malcolm

And to the Lord Jesus Christ who, Mavis
and I believe, made it all possible.

Table of Contents

Chapter 1

It all started as a normal day often does.

June 15th 2004.

It started like any other day really. It was hot and both Mavis and I had been working in the small bedroom we called the office. Spirits were high. Just six months earlier Mavis and I had started a new business. A little late in life perhaps, as Mavis was one year after her retiring age of 60 and I was her toy boy of 59. We had decided that a business venture might be worth considering because Ailsa, our second daughter, had been selling wedding gowns for the last ten years and wanted to do something a little different with the designs. We had discussed it at length and she had prepared some new designs, which, after a great deal of research, we had made in China. The idea was that these wedding gowns could be sold, not only in Ailsa's shop, but also through a chain of stockists we would establish throughout the UK. My job was sales and Mavis's job was everything else, as that seemed a fair division of labour. The business had been doing very well. We were up over 80% on forecast and the future looked bright.

As well as making appointments for me and looking after the paperwork, Mavis also looked after Helen her stepmother. She had lived with us all our married life and at 83, was becoming frail.

Mavis and I had been married 37 years and over the last 10 we had worked together running an Opticians business. Mavis had been a teacher but in 1980 developed ME and could not stay awake for more than five minutes, let alone teach. Her recovery had been very slow, but steady, and after nearly five years, she was able to do little things. As time progressed, and as we needed a little help at work, Mavis started to work for me part time. Slowly, as she felt more able, she eased her way back into full time employment and in many ways took over the day-to-day running of the business, allowing me to concentrate on expansion plans, etc. We had worked together well over the years, each complementing the other. As in our marriage we became a solid team, each knowing how the other ticked, when to lead or when the other needed support.

It was nearly VAT quarter end, and so it was time to balance the books. The office was hot, especially so for Sunderland, and we made it even hotter by sweating over the spreadsheets Mavis had set up, trying to ensure everything was right for our second VAT return. Did we have this amount in the right column? Neither of us were completely sure but we stood our own ground until one managed to convince the other which of us was correct. Six o'clock approached and after several heated discussions, we decided it was time for something to eat and to stop for the day. We came downstairs into the kitchen and Mavis started preparing the dinner (a salad as the weather was hot). Meanwhile, I changed the filter on the water tap, which seemed to have become so slow that evaporation from the kettle would have produced water faster. Mavis finished the preparation and we all sat down to eat. The new tap filter had to be washed for at least 5 minutes to make sure any residue was removed, and we were quite happy for this to happen as we sat eating. Ours was a small kitchen/dinette with a table that sat four against the wall so I always "climbed in" and Mavis sat on the end with Helen opposite. After about 5 minutes, I asked Mavis if she would switch off the tap as she was nearest. I thought it a bit strange that I did not get any response, so I said it again. There was still no response. This time I nudged Mavis and asked her again. Nothing! I peered round at her, and although her mouth was still chewing, her eyes were fixed. It was clear that 'nobody was at home.' Helen had not noticed anything untoward so I think she was quite shocked when I jumped over Mavis and ran for the telephone. I had some first aid knowledge and although I had never seen one before, I suspected a stroke, I just did not realised how serious. The 999 call made, I immediately made another to our neighbours Bill and Pat a few doors away. We had been very good friends since I first moved to the North East from London in 1965. Fortunately, they were in and Pat came to look after Helen so that I could go with Mavis to the hospital. It was 19:00 on Tuesday 15th June.

Time seemed to twist itself in those vital minutes when awaiting the ambulance's arrival. Pat took Helen into the lounge while I stayed with Mavis, who was still sitting upright within the confines of the table. I left her there as she didn't seem to be in any danger but, as she still seemed to be trying to chew her food, I removed it to stop her choking. We then waited for the ambulance which drew up outside very quietly and two paramedics came into the house and took over. After an initial assessment, they carried Mavis to the ambulance and I watched as they tried to find a vein for an injection. Unfortunately, the body had already started to close down and so reluctantly, after about 10 minutes, they gave up and said they were taking Mavis to the Accident and Emergency department at Sunderland Royal City Hospital and that I should follow by car. I went back into the house, told Pat what was happening, and explained to Helen the best way I could. I hoped that she would not become too upset and would just prepare herself for bed as normal.

I arrived at the hospital just after the ambulance and thinking that I would be there for some time, parked outside the hospital grounds in order to avoid the exorbitant parking charges, and ran for A & E. After announcing myself to reception I sat and waited, trying to take in exactly what had happened and preparing for what was likely to happen next. After what seemed like an eternity, I heard my name called. I was ushered into a large room with Mavis lying on what looked like an operating table with various nurses and doctors looking after her, or so I thought. The discussion went something along these lines:

Doctor "I am getting a very strange reading on the ECG machine. Are you sure it is connected properly?"

Nurse: "Yes of course it is.

Doctor": Are you sure?"

Nurse: "Yes Of course I am sure. If you have any doubts come and check it yourself."

The Doctor looked at the ECG machine again and went closer to Mavis to check. At this time I think they had forgotten I was in the room as the Doctor set great store by showing the nurse how each contact point of the ECG machine should be connected properly. It seemed that the sensors that should have been put on the arms had been put on the legs, and vice-versa. All this time Mavis was still unconscious and I was still wondering exactly what was going on. About five minutes later, the doctor came over and confirmed that they thought Mavis had had a stroke and the next stage was to find out what sort of stroke it was, either a clot or a bleed. The only way of achieving this was by a CAT scan and Mavis would be taken down as soon as possible.

Mavis seemed to be given to strong movements, as if she was in pain, but not 'fitting' as such. Here started the next problem. As Mavis kept on moving, the Doctor decided that they could not do a scan until she became quieter. After about 30 minutes, this still had not happened, so they decided they would have to summon an anaesthetist to subdue her during the scan. Problem No 2 was that because it was after 6 o'clock all the anaesthetists had gone home and the one on call lived in Jesmond, nearly 13 miles away. Therefore, we waited. I was shown into a waiting room and told that I could use the telephone if I wanted to inform relatives. Fortunately, I had my mobile telephone with me, which had all the numbers I needed, so I started dialling.

The first was to Heather, our eldest daughter, who is married with three young children and lives in Derby. I remember it ringing and then clicking onto the answer phone. "They can't be out," I shouted in my frustration; they have small children; they have to be in. I put the receiver down and started to dial again, as maybe I had dialled the wrong number. Still the same response. It then dawned on me that it was Tuesday. Heather and Mike have their house group meeting on a Tuesday. This is where small groups of people from the church would meet for prayer and discussion. They always put the answer phone on to avoid interruptions. If only I could get through, they would all be praying for various things, but not for my Mavis who really needed all the prayers everyone could muster. I would leave a message asking Heather to ring me on the mobile as soon as she could but not wishing to alarm her too much.

I now tried ringing Ailsa, our other daughter, who lives in Carlisle, about 80 miles away. Again the answer phone! What was happening to my family? When I am watching something very interesting on the television, they always ring me just at the most exciting or interesting point and yet, when I need to contact them, they are unavailable. I consoled myself with the fact that Ailsa at least would have her mobile with her, which was always on. "The mobile that you are trying to reach is switched off. Please try later," came the response. Stay calm I told myself. OK I would leave the same message and hope one of them would ring me back.

I went back into the ward unit and asked the nurse what, if anything, was happening. She said that the anaesthetist had arrived and they were going to put Mavis under so they could get an accurate image from the scan. As she was speaking, Mavis on a trolley with an entourage of people passed slowly down the corridor and out of sight.

Why these pages?

During the writing of this book I have been asked various question many times and they have ranged over a multitude of subjects. I found it difficult to try to include the answers in a way that would not spoil the flow of Mavis's story and therefore these questions will attempted to be answered in the framed pages like this one, in between chapters. I hope by the end they will answer most if not all of your questions.

Chapter 2
Despair.

We have been extremely fortunate in our life with having lovely loyal friends. It started when Mavis went to teacher training college in Birmingham, in 1963. I met Mavis there and six of her friends who seemed inseparable; only later I learnt that this was because they shared a strong Christian faith. The girls later married Christian men and they settled all over the country. The men have also become close friends, so we have all kept in touch. We are probably closest to Margaret and Keith through the years as they live in Bridlington and are the nearest in travelling time. Keith and I also share similar philosophies on life. I decided to ring them. It was now about 10 o'clock and still there was no news of Mavis. Margaret answered the telephone. At last someone to talk to; the first person with whom I could actually share what had happened. I could hear the shock in her voice but all I could tell her was that Mavis had had a stroke. I did not know any other details at all, which was very frustrating. To save using the phone in the hospital Margaret agreed to phone the rest of our friends to let them know. That was my duty done. I had tried to contact all those who needed to know. Why wasn't the hospital telling me anything? I tried Heather again and this time she answered as the House Group had just finished. I explained the best I could and left it at that. She said she would keep trying Ailsa until she eventually made contact. For me it was back to feeling helpless. The endless wait.

Wednesday 16th June 2004.

00:30 I received a call from the doctor and I was taken to a small room. He asked me to sit down. My stomach churned as I waited for him to begin. Mavis had had her scan and was now on the assessment ward. It was not good news. She had had a very serious stroke. It was a clot, not a bleed, so they were not going to move her to Newcastle for more specialist treatment. Unfortunately by the time they had managed to do the scan it had become too late to inject her with the clot busting drugs we have all read about. The doctor even went so far as to say that they did not believe in using them anyway, as the side effects were considerable. Therefore, nearly six hours after it had happened, the truth was eventually dawning. Mavis was lying in a ward still unconscious and there did not seem to be anything the hospital or I could do about it. I summoned up the courage to ask what the prognosis was. "Not good", he replied and suggested that I ought to contact the family to decide what we wanted to do with Mavis's organs. At 01:00 I left the hospital and walked back to the lonely car parked in the street. My head was whirling with all this information because I needed to know, but somehow did not want to.

Bill and Pat were awaiting my return. I tried to explain concisely what had happened and they left to go to their beds together. I went to my empty bed and prayed to my God whom I knew could do something about it if he wanted to. Would he? Nobody knew, but I was sure everyone that had heard the news so far would be praying that he would.

07:00. I woke up, felt the emptiness in the bed, and realised it had not been a nightmare after all. I rang Heather who told me she had managed to contact Ailsa and that Ailsa was coming over early to the hospital. Heather said she would be travelling up later in the day once she had managed to arrange for child sitting etc. I went to make sure Helen was Ok and explained to her exactly what I knew. I cannot imagine what she thought. The person who had looked after her ever since she became incapable of managing things for herself was now no longer available, and all that responsibility had been passed to me. Ours had been a fiery relationship at times but I think she knew I would do my best for her. For now however, all that had to be put on hold and she needed to look after herself the best she could, for a few hours anyway, until I sorted things out.

I rang the rest of the family to keep everyone informed. Then I rang Cathy, a particular friend in another church. Cathy had always impressed me with her closeness to God and I asked her to pray for Mavis. The wonderful thing about the Christian family is that if you have a need, everyone will help the best way they can. Cathy said not only would she pray but she would also inform others so that a prayer chain would be formed. Within 24 hours of Mavis having her stroke, people in 10 different countries were praying to God asking for his will to be done, although at this juncture nobody knew what God's will was. I also rang the Reverend John Boyers, Mavis's cousin's husband, with whom I had formed a good rapport with over the years. He asked did I mind if he prayed for us over the telephone. I said I didn't but asked, "What are we going to pray for?" "That God's will be done," he said.

I arrived back at the hospital just after nine and eventually found the ward to which Mavis had been moved. I always think that when you take a person into hospital you should be given a card that you can put into a machine at any time, which would tell you exactly where that patient has been allocated. Something similar to the tracker system they have on cars, but for patients.

Mavis was in bed and I sat beside her hoping against hope that she was Ok. At least she was still alive, but for how long?

The doctor came to tell me that unexpectedly she had survived the night and had not had any further strokes. She was still on the critical list but there was at least a little hope. The next fortnight was going to be critical, as it was likely that if anything else happened she would not survive. In the meantime, they would try to transfer her to the specialist stroke ward as soon as possible. I tried speaking to Mavis but received no response, and at about 10:30 Ailsa arrived. Heather arrived at 13:00 and we sat and discussed and waited and discussed and waited and discussed. We were there but why? Was it because we thought we had to be - just in case Mavis suddenly woke up and everything was going to be Ok? We knew it wasn't, but in this grey limbo land none of us wanted to explore the thoughts that we were probably there to say goodbye.

15:30 Apart from the nurses doing checks and observations every 15 minutes, the time had been spent talking among ourselves, then the ward sister with the doctor came to say that a place had become available in the specialist stroke ward D41, and that if we wished, Mavis could be moved there. Wow, a specialist stroke ward! This could only aid Mavis's recovery, couldn't it?

At 18:15, a new nurse came to move Mavis. We followed him to a small side room close to the Nursing station. We then noticed liquid all over the floor and asked the nurse why. He investigated and found it to be Mavis's urine that had leaked from the bottle, because the catheter had not been attached properly. Had we known that this was an omen, we might have requested that Mavis be moved back on to the general ward from where she had just come.

Unless it has happened to you or someone you know, you have very little idea of what is going on, how the person that has had the stroke is expected to respond and how serious things are. What you do expect is to be given every opportunity both for the patient to recover and for you and the family to cope with what has happened. Initially in ward D41, this did not happen. We felt that the attitude was that we were a nuisance to be endured, rather than a patient and family to be helped. What happened over the next 10 weeks would try everyone's patience to the highest level and unfortunately, Mavis would be at the centre of it.

My background.

I was not brought up in a Christian home and therefore found my own faith. As I suspect most of us did, or do at times, as a child I used to pray to God. My prayers included everything from passing my exams at school, to getting me out of the unhappy circumstances I found myself in when my mother and father split up when I was fifteen. I think I was on the way to believing in a God when I first met Mavis. As I was a boy scout in London, we had to attend church once a month for the Church parade, and so I became familiar with church activities and even joined the choir of the church in Streatham. They also had a young people's group called the Sixty Society that I attended for both companionship and various social activities. I had left home and was living with some good friends who had taken me in when I arrived on their doorstep one night at about 22:30. Essentially, at the age of sixteen I was a free agent, and did what I wanted, when I wanted. This I had done for a couple of years and after buying a car before I could drive, I started going out with a girl from the church who already had a full driving licence. She was training to be a teacher in Birmingham, and so we only saw each other when she returned home for the holidays or when I went to visit her at college. It was during one such visit that I met Mavis. Margaret dumped me and Mavis initially took pity on me I think, and so started a friendship with her that has lasted all my life.

Chapter 3.

Optimism returns.

Thursday 17th June 2004.

Another day another dawn. Ailsa had gone home the night before. Heather had arranged to have the rest of the week off and someone to look after the children. It is very strange at times to see how different children both from the same parents and with the same upbringing can cope with things so differently. Heather had gone, probably like me, into pragmatic mode. Ailsa, on the other hand, whilst not falling to pieces, was finding it very much harder to cope. She was also supposed to be going to Barcelona on business the next day, so would she go?

It was a comfort to have Heather stopping here with me as she could talk to Helen at home and give me the benefit of some of her wisdom. The morning passed in a busy ward atmosphere. Checks were made every 15 minutes and nurses came into the room to remake the bed and change Mavis's position.

This afternoon we had a response. Mavis opened her eyes, tried to smile, and then went away again. I use the word 'away' advisably because it was not sleep. It was just as if the brain had signalled her to join us for a few seconds and had then left without another thought. The first thing both Heather and I noticed was that not all her face smiled. Only the right side moved and then only a little. The left had dropped and it made Mavis look hollow and very ill. Of course, we wanted her to survive didn't we? If half her face was not working what other parts would not be working? If she did survive what quality of life could she expect, if any? Didn't anyone have any answers? We asked anyone who would listen but everyone said exactly the same thing, it was too early to tell and they would know more after they had done another scan. That was fine for them; they had seen it all before, but we hadn't. It was strange and somehow frightening. Being frightened by the unknown is something we humans seem to do more regularly than being afraid of the real thing.

Friday 18th June 2004.

This morning Heather and I decided to split the day. She would go in early to see if there was any improvement and I would stay at home to tidy up the business details that needed sorting, including the VAT return, then go to the hospital in the afternoon. Ailsa would be there anyway so it would be good for the girls to spend some time on their own to talk without me there.

I went to see Helen, but there was something strange this morning as she was usually up around nine and it was now much later. I tried to speak to her, but what response I did get, made no sense. Would the ambulance service think I was just playing around with hoax calls if I rang again saying somebody else in the house had had a stroke? I dialled anyway and they came very quickly. At about 12 noon Helen was admitted to the same hospital having also suffered a stroke. She had had mini strokes before called TIAs so this time the symptoms were recognisable. We expected her to return to normal quickly but after checking her out on the ward, it was agreed that she had had a more serious stroke than before. Nothing catastrophic but they would keep her in for a few days to keep an eye on her.

The vigil started. We went into the hospital to see Mavis then upstairs, two flights, to see Helen, then back downstairs to see Mavis again. All the staff were sworn to secrecy on Mavis's ward as the doctors thought it best that she didn't get an inkling that Helen was also in hospital having suffered a stroke - and was sleeping twenty feet above her head on the next floor up.

I returned home with Heather so not technically to an empty house. Life had changed but it still had not sunk in just how much. I was more concerned that the bed felt cold and empty. The fact was that it was going to be like that for a very long time, if not forever. I wondered how Ailsa was doing. She was supposed to be going to Barcelona this weekend on business, but trying to persuade her to go was a major exercise. Understandably, she didn't want to leave her Mum just in case something happened, but what could she do if she stayed? Mavis was stable and all we could do was to sit by the bedside. Reluctantly, she agreed to go, provided we kept her informed of any change. Text messages still kept coming from Barcelona nearly every hour checking that things were Ok for both her Mum and her Gran.

Saturday 19th June 2004.

There was not much point rushing into the hospital. Only emergency doctors were on call today and therefore the wards just ticked over. Nobody would do anything for either for Mavis or Helen until the following week. Heather would go in to see both Helen and Mavis so it was time to do some more work for the business. I was worried that anyone ringing the company would have only received the answer phone message and very often, this usually meant that a company is in difficulties. Although I realised there was now a problem, I did not want to broadcast it this way.

Now for the sentimental side. The message on the answer phone used Mavis's voice. It had taken a long time to get it right and I could remember the fun and frustration of making it sound correct in the time available. So, should I change the message, which somehow did not seem appropriate or should I write to all the stockists explaining the situation? I decided that it was better to write to the stockists and let them know what had happened and more particularly that the message on the answer phone would stay, because it was my Mavis's voice and I liked to listen to it.

Margaret and Keith, our friends from Bridlington, came to visit and were shocked at Mavis's condition. Keith remarked that Mavis looked so bad that he really didn't think she would survive. He qualified this by saying "There was just nothing there and the face was so distorted that it seemed hard to imagine that even if Mavis did survive, she could improve sufficiently to have any quality of life."

Monday 21st June 2004.

I arrived at the hospital early as I thought that with the start of a new week everyone would be keen to take more tests and expurgate things. Helen was fine sitting up in bed, rather enjoying the attention, and wondering where she was. Although the stroke had not damaged her mobility of her body, it had destroyed many more of her memory cells. So no matter how hard I tried to explain to Helen, she was sure she was in a hotel and the 'servants' were being really nice to her. I went down to Mavis's ward and asked what was happening to her. They said that they would try to have Mavis up today and that the speech therapist was coming later to assess her. Up until this time, she had been on a drip and had been in bed all the time so for something fresh to happen it had to be good. The speech therapist came while I was seeing Helen again and so I do not know exactly what she did or how Mavis was assessed; enough to say that a notice was put over the bed informing everyone that soft food only was allowed as Mavis's swallowing capacity had been severely reduced. They did not want to take the chance of her choking. Mavis winced every time she moved or was moved and I asked her a series of question to try to establish why. By slowly mentioning nearly every part of her body we eventually established by shakes or nods that she was complaining of back pain, but we put it down to the fact that she had been lying in bed for so long.

Tuesday 22nd June 2004 .

Mavis is a little more aware today and everyone thinks it would be a good idea if she could start to feed herself for the first time since her stroke. It would have been, if they had given her clean cutlery to use instead of the fork with another person's dried food remains still between the prongs! All the time staff are saying Mavis must drink more fluids and we must encourage Mavis to drink as much as possible. It does not take a genius to notice that for a bed bound patient to take fluids, they must be able to reach them! Mavis's drinks always seemed to be left at the bottom of the bed, well out of her reach. During the afternoon Mavis was put on a hoist and transferred to a large armchair in the room for about 30 minutes before being put back into bed. Mavis signalled to me that the top of her leg was hurting and I investigated to see sores developing between the top of the leg and the body. Calling a nurse, I suggested a cream might help relieve the soreness and that, while doing all the monitoring that they were supposed to carry out, surely a simple inspection to check and respond to the start of bedsores would not have been too much to expect. She agreed and said that they would take care of it, but I wondered if it would really happen.

At this point we could see Mavis trying to stay awake but she still didn't say anything and what started as a day full of optimism eventually closed with very little being achieved.

Wednesday 23rd June 2004.

Today became the highlight of the week. After each visit, I would always leave the room by saying "I Love you" and, in the past, either had no, or very little response. This time, just before going home, I said the words and got a very soft but just audible "I love you" back. My heart raced as I drove home. Something was happening to Mavis's brain and there was an improvement. Would it continue? To be honest I did not want to speculate about it. The fact that Mavis responded for the first time in over a week was so significant to me that I could think of nothing else. What a contrast to my feelings only 24 hours previously.

Thursday 24th June 2006.

Today was also going to see the discharge of Helen, so time would have to be spent with her at home, and I made the decision that my time had to be more organised. I decided that I would go to the hospital early in the mornings and stay until lunchtime. Then I would go home to ensure Helen was up, dressed and otherwise Ok before making her lunch. I would then do about two hours work before returning to the hospital at about 14:30; stay until about 17:00 then going home to feed Helen and myself. I would then go back to the hospital for the evening shift. Once home again, I could do all the paperwork needed before going to bed. Of course, what really happened is that I made a habit of calling in at Bill and Pats to update then, sit drinking their coffee until the small hours and then attempt to do the paperwork at three in the morning.

Unfortunately, for Helen, she had relapsed a little and the hospital insisted she stay in so they could keep her under observation.

Meanwhile Mavis had had her CT scan and the Professor who was looking after her was happy to talk to me about it. He told me that in many ways Mavis had been unfortunate for although the clot was small it had struck at the very centre of the brain affecting quite a large area. I asked him what the prognosis was and he told me that although it was too early to tell, as a general rule 80% of any impairment returns within the first 3 weeks. He kept emphasising that Mavis's stoke had been very serious indeed. I also mentioned at this point that Mavis had had to leave teaching some 20 years previously because she had contracted ME and that had effectively closed the brain down for nearly 3 years. As I did not get much response to that information, I concluded that he was one of those doctors who did not believe in ME.

We also met 'F' the Physiotherapist for the first time. She advised that Mavis was too fatigued to start any physio but to make sure that the left arm, which was still immobile, should be supported at all times. As I went home in the afternoon, the neighbours were outside talking, and I was able to give them all an update in one go. I particularly mentioned the response I had received from Mavis last night and I noticed that we all had a little cry of joy. Even more sentimental, as this time it included me!

Saturday 26th June 2004.

Heather was popping up for the day and it was lovely to see her. As well as being a super daughter, she is also an Occupational Therapist, (OT) within the NHS. Hopefully, she would have a slightly better insight into the workings of the NHS. So far, I am feeling both frustrated and annoyed at what seems or, more importantly, what seems NOT to be happening. I waited for Heather to come, which gave me the opportunity of a lie in, and we both arrived at the hospital about 11:30. Mavis was sleeping as usual and so we had the chance to study her chart at the bottom of the bed. It said two things that began to disturb me. One was that many meals were being refused and two that no bowel movements had been recorded.

It was lunchtime and the meal arrived. I woke Mavis to tell her and asked her why so many of the previous meals had been refused. She was so fatigued she could not even answer and it then became clear that she was not refusing her slops it was just that she was too tired to eat and nobody was helping her! We also notice that Mavis is in a lot of discomfort from her catheter and so we asked the nurses to do something about it. We also asked them to find out why they do not seem to be recording any bowel movements. Unfortunately, Heather is not able to wave her magic wand and therefore returns to Derby as concerned as me about her Mum's care.

Sunday 27th June 2004.

I decided to go to the church that Cathy goes to this morning. We have many good friends there who I knew were still praying for Mavis.

The only way they would get to know if their prayers were being answered would be by getting an update. It felt very strange going into the church by myself, but they had always been a warm congregation and I managed to see Cathy before the service started. As prayer secretary for the church, Cathy stood up at the end of the service and gave everyone the update asking them to keep on praying. Yes, Mavis was still alive but she still had a very long way to go if she was not going to become a vegetable.

This afternoon Mavis seemed to have a little more energy so perhaps something had prompted some sort of response in the brain although I doubt if she was aware of what. She now seemed able to stay awake for 15 minutes at a time and if you asked her a question in the right way you could get a simple "Yes" or "No" answer. It was through this Gestapo type interrogation that it began to dawn on me that Mavis had very serious problems. She knew who I was but could not say my name. I think she recognised Ailsa and Heather, but that was all. She had no memory of what had happened, and the stroke had wiped out almost all her other memory. She could not tell the time, didn't know where she lived and had no concept of what day it was or what was wrong with her, let alone the name of the prime minister. The left side of her body was totally paralysed; her face was twisted and strange, like suffering from Bells Palsy. Although she had worn spectacles since she was a small child, she now would not wear them. Her day was spent sleeping either in the bed or in the chair, if the staff had lifted her on to it.

A Nurse came to take blood sugar levels, pricked Mavis's finger on her good hand without cleaning it and said she had to inform the doctor that the blood sugar level is 13, far higher than it should be. Having watched the exercise, I suggested she might like to take it again after cleaning the finger as Mavis had just finished sipping a drink of 'high juice' from a cup. She assured me it would not make any difference but, after I insisted, she reluctantly took it again. The sugar level is now determined to be 8.7. This level of incompetence worried me. Panic over, but now even more disconcerting, I find slightly moist tablets on Mavis's chest when the Nurse has gone and can only conclude that these have dropped out from the paralysed side of Mavis's mouth, without the staff noticing. Surely, they have a responsibility to ensure patients are able to take their medication. What is the point of having medication prescribed if no one ensures it is taken? I begin to question seriously if Mavis should be in this ward at all, but what else could we do? After all, they are supposed to be the experts, aren't they? Mavis is still very uncomfortable with the catheter and I wondered if anything had been done about it.

Monday 28th June 2004.

The professor who has been looking after Mavis since her first admittance to the ward always said that Mavis was not really his patient and that she would be under the wing of a Dr. O. She had been away on holiday but was due to return today, so I went to the hospital early as usual and awaited the normal ward rounds. Mavis had now been moved from the small private room to a room in the main ward that had four bays and each bay contained six beds. I wondered if it was because I had complained. The catheter had been replaced but was still very uncomfortable. I asked the nurse to check yet again and while she was doing that, I read the notices scattered around the ward. On each bay was a notice informing visitors of visiting times, and stipulating that should anyone be requested to leave the ward they must comply. To refuse would constitute a trespass and therefore you could be removed by force if necessary. I sat with Mavis as the new Doctor and her entourage of assistants and nurses crept around the bays until she came into Mavis's bay, and asked me to leave. I can't put into words how shocked I was. Here was this Doctor asking me to leave my wife who could say very little and understand or remember even less! I knew I could not refuse, as I would invoke their trespass rule, so I simply replied, "I prefer to stay." She replied that I must leave as she was going to examine my wife. My retort was that I would see nothing that I had not seen before and therefore why couldn't I stay? This standoff lasted nearly 15 minutes and I was beginning to think I would be ejected at any moment by some big security guard. All the junior doctors and nurses were looking very embarrassed but I was determined to stand my ground.

At this point Mavis woke up and to everyone's amazement spluttered the words "He stays." This was a pivotal point in the debate. The only other reason the doctor could find for me to leave was that other patients' confidentiality might be compromised if I stayed on the ward. As Mavis was the first on the bay to be seen, it seemed a compromise that I should stay until Mavis had been seen. Then I would leave immediately so that they could go on and examine the other patients. Reluctantly agreeing to this compromise, she examined Mavis, asked a few questions which Mavis could not answer and therefore I had to, and then I left. Afterwards when she had finished her rounds she came up to me and said tersely, "I hold clinics every Wednesday afternoon for any relative who wants to ask me questions. If you want any more information I suggest you attend then!" I asked what time would be suitable and she told me 16:00.

In the afternoon, I returned to the ward and saw that nothing new had been written on Mavis's chart. There was also still no mention of any bowel movements, so I think it is about time I become more active in Mavis's well being. I asked a nurse to investigate and she confirmed that Mavis has had no bowel movement since being admitted. That meant 13 days of constipation. Before her stroke, you could set Big Ben by Mavis's bowels so I suggested something ought to be done. I am told however, that this lack of movement is very common with stroke patients and therefore the Doctor would not do anything for at least another 2 days. Maybe she saw the disbelief on my face or heard the anger in my voice, who can tell, but at 18:00, another Nurse appeared saying now that yes, Mavis could have treatment for her constipation and she will be given a pill at 22:00. It is rather late but I considered it was worthwhile staying in the Ward to ensure Mavis received it. It arrived two hours early so I think they wanted to be rid of me. They offered Mavis a drink to take the tablet and the nurse went to mark it down on the chart. After studying the chart for a few moments, the nurse now asked *me* to tell *her* if I knew what fluids Mavis has had during the day as nobody had bothered to record it.

Tuesday 29th June 2004.

I arrived early to make sure Mavis was fed and after breakfast, Mavis was put into a big blue chair that looked like befriending her for the rest of her days in hospital. She was put in it at 10:00 and seemed destined to remain in it forever. I fed her lunch and returned home in the afternoon as I still had several things to accomplish at work. Returning in the evening at about 20:15 I could see Mavis was still in the chair and extremely uncomfortable. The left arm was still not supported and it was left dangling down over the side of the chair. It must have been like that for some time as it had become stuck to the vinyl. The arm was very cold and slightly swollen. I asked a nurse if Mavis could be returned to bed. As nothing happened, at around 21:00 I went to find another nurse to ask again. I was yelled at that the nursing staff had other patients to attend to besides Mavis. Eventually two nurses appeared and using the hoist put Mavis back to bed. I was now told in no uncertain manner that I had to leave and that Mavis had been asked twice during the day if she wanted to go back to bed but had refused. I could not believe this to be true as Mavis was sleeping nearly all the day and it was more comfortable to sleep in a bed than in a vinyl chair.

So now what do you do? It is obvious that the level of care is quite unacceptable and the nursing skills leave much to be desired. If I complained, would they take it out on Mavis or would things improve? As it happened, I went for a drink and got talking to another family that told me the wife had had four strokes now on separate occasions. Each time they had experienced a similar lack of nursing and care. They said, now, whenever the wife had a stroke the ambulance took her into hospital and as soon as she had stabilised the family took her home and managed the caring there. It did cross my mind to do the same but how could I transport Mavis home and, if I could, how would I lift her into the house or up the stairs to bed, not to mention to the toilet? I went back to the ward and spoke to the doctor stressing my concerns. He advised me to take it up with the senior nurse on duty. I also asked him to look again at the level of laxative that Mavis was on as either she was still constipated or the bowel movements were not being recorded!

Wednesday 30th June 2004.

After Monday's confrontation with Dr. O., I was itching for 16:00 to arrive so that I could ask her all the questions and increasing doubts that were escalating in my mind. I arrived at the room especially selected for the Doctor's clinics exactly on time, hoping she would be able to give me some answers, to find nobody else there. Determined not to be beaten into submission by this jumped up prima donna, I resolved to wait at least until 20:00 by which time I assumed she would have gone home. At 18:30, she arrived without any apology and repeatedly said that she did not know the answer to any of the questions I asked. I am not sure whether anything at all had been achieved apart from the waste of my time

22

Thursday July 1st 2004.

Our Wedding Anniversary. I have always remembered our Wedding Anniversary and so had Mavis, but this year she had no idea what this was. Ailsa brought an anniversary card in with her and guided Mavis's right hand to write it. I am not sure whether the sentiments she wrote were all hers or what Ailsa thought Mavis would have said, but it was very precious and even if Mavis did not survive, at least I knew she loved me. The physio arrived again to make an initial assessment and Mavis was lifted by hoist from the bed to the big chair at the side of the bed. I do not think Mavis could have cared less; everything seemed to be such an effort for the brain let alone the body. The physio left and Mavis was left in the care of the nurses to wash. I noticed the Urine bag was still on the floor for people to tread on so I picked it up and put it in a bowl to protect both the bag and Mavis. I also noticed the left arm was left hanging unsupported over the side of the chair again. My goodness what would happen if I could not be there? However when I had arrived at 08:30 to make sure Mavis was being fed, I remembered noticing that her urine bag was on the floor and empty then. I had replaced it on its hanger and assumed that it must just have been emptied. I had gone home at 11:00 and returned at 13:00 to make sure Mavis had her lunch. Again, the urine bag was empty. This is good I thought, maybe complaining to the nurse has had some effect and Mavis was now getting the attention to which all patients are entitled. After lunch, I left again, coming back at 16:30 to note the urine bag was still empty so I think it best to check the chart, and low and behold, no urine has been recorded during the day. I reported this to a nurse who examined Mavis to discover that the catheter has been blocked and in fact, nobody had emptied the bag all day. This meant that Mavis had been unable to pass urine all day whilst consistently Ailsa and I had been doing our best to encourage her to take fluids.

It was now evening mealtime and once again, I returned the entire cutlery because it was filthy. I asked the nurse why the urine output had not been monitored and she accepted that it should have been but the staff were far too busy. I also noted to the nurse that unless the record keeping had again not been done, Mavis was still constipated. She agreed and said she would note it in the doctors' book. She also told me that the skin on Mavis's buttocks was beginning to break down now and that they would have to remove the catheter. What a way to spend a wedding anniversary! This was only 16 days after being admitted so what was the rest of the duration of Mavis's stay going to deteriorate into? We asked various questions from the staff but nobody was interested and in fact, one nurse was quite rude, more or less telling me to mind my own business as the care of the patient was their responsibility not mine and what did I know anyway? If only they would take responsibility for the patient, I would NOT have to spend all day at the hospital and keep asking questions!

Ailsa had gone upstairs to see Helen and talked over the situation with the sister of Helen's ward. When she came back down, we discussed it carefully and decided that we just had to complain and take the risk that Mavis might suffer, as after all, she was suffering now, and we were not doing anything. I was so annoyed now that I went to complain to the highest level on the ward and said I would be giving a copy of all my complaints to her in the morning. I said goodnight and went home to write them. (Appendix 1)

Friday 2nd July 2004.

I handed in my list of complaints to the charge nurse, who read them through and asked me what I was going to do next? There is still a fear that if you complain too much the patient that is supposedly in their care is going to suffer more if you complain than if you don't. Therefore, I tried to offer a little gesture of goodwill and reconciliation by saying that I will not take it any further if things improve. I didn't want to cause a fuss I just wanted my Mavis looked after properly, because at this point in time she is unable to look after herself and I can't do it all for her.

Mavis's Background.

Mavis was born in Sunderland into a Christian home. She was an only child but as with so many northern families enjoyed a rich upbringing in the company of her close cousins as often they would live in the same street, even in the same house. Mavis's mother died when she was 14 and she took over the house responsibilities. Her father remarried just as Mavis was taking her A levels and Mavis decided she would like to go away to college. She went to Birmingham to study to become a teacher but at one time had very serious intentions of becoming a missionary when her training was finished. At college she was known as Miv, the tea and post girl, as she was always the one up early and inevitably collected the post and put the kettle on.

When Mavis left college, she returned to her home in Sunderland and, as this meant we were over 300 miles away from each other, we decided that it was time to call it a day. As a last farewell, she invited me up to spend Christmas with her and her family. Just before Christmas 1965 I arrived and on the 28th December, her father was killed and Helen, her stepmother, was seriously injured in a road accident. I gave up my job in London and moved North to help Mavis in any way I could. It was through going to church with Mavis that I went to a Billy Graham mission and decided that there was a God and to give my life to him. I was baptised in 1966 and Mavis and I were married in July 1967.

Chapter 4
Changes at last.

Sunday 4th July 2004.

About 9:30, there was a noise just outside the ward. It was difficult to make out, but it was music, and it seemed to be music that Mavis and I were familiar with. We listened more intently and it seemed to be hymns. I asked the nursing staff if they could put Mavis into her big blue chair. This takes an age but after it is done, I pushed Mavis towards where the music was coming from. It was just outside the ward and the Salvation Army had come to play. They were just the other side of the doors but the ward doors opened outwards so we could not open the doors to hear it any better. A small group of patients gathered round the doors singing and trying to join in the best they could. We arrived at the doors for the last verse of the last hymn. Mavis burst into tears and we go back to the bed. Why had she cried? I did not know and she could not tell me! After lunch, I tried again. What had caused the grief? It transpired that it was a mixture of feelings. Helplessness of both body and brain, total dependency on others and unable to get to church to worship, had all welled up into a huge emotion that had eventually come out. Although the grief was very sad to behold it told me that Mavis was now, probably for the first time, becoming aware of her situation. In some ways, this was good but the despair that it showed was something I had not bargained for.

Monday 5th July 2004.

Ward round again this morning, and I am allowed to sit in on the same understanding as last week - that I leave the minute they have finished with Mavis. This is fine but this time we are told that Mavis might be moving to Monkwearmouth, a different hospital that might be able to provide better rehabilitation. As they did not take everyone, Mavis would have to be assessed by the consultant in charge of the ward and he would probably come sometime this week or next. Something to look forward to.

Thursday 8th July 2004.

The physio seems to be taking an active interest in Mavis now although the sessions are only twice a week and then only for about twenty minutes, but at least something appears to be happening. Up until now, Mavis's physio sessions have been based in the chair but today they have decided that Mavis was going to go to the physio room. The big blue chair was pushed with great difficulty through the ward doors and into the physio room. Today was going to be Mavis's big day. They were going to lift Mavis upright, albeit with a hoist. It worked well, a bit like a large baby bouncer; in fact, it was exactly that, for Mavis was just like a big baby at this stage. She had no memory and very little language, difficulty feeding herself, difficulty swallowing, had no control over her urine output and, if she wasn't still been constipated who knows how her bowels would have behaved! Mavis stood in the hoist for about 2 minutes and was then lowered back to the blue chair and returned to the ward.

We are told that the consultant will visit sometime today and with great anticipation, we waited. I took our minds off things by doing more exercises. My name is... I live at................ My telephone number is..., but received very little response. If Mavis does not regain much more memory than she has now, if she is ever lost, nobody will know where to return her to. The consultant arrived in the afternoon and goes through his own evaluation including a general physical examination and various mental tests. Maybe we were expecting too much but after about 45 minutes, he concluded that Mavis is not ready to go to Monkwearmouth and bitter disappointment sets in. He did say however, that he would come and reassess the situation in two weeks time, so something to aim for. Heather is coming up again this weekend and I hope that she can advise me on some ways I might be able to help Mavis. After all, if I am having to spend all my time at the hospital to make sure she received the attention she deserved the least I could do was to make myself useful. I would let Heather do her assessment over the weekend. I think in many ways she is just as much in the dark as I am but it helps to talk to a professional whose crystal ball is no better than mine is. She was an outpatient OT and although not having any direct contact with stroke survivors she had seen the way other people responded to treatment.

Saturday and Sunday 10th & 11th July 2004.

Heather has been here this weekend and is delighted to see how much her Mum has improved. I suppose being too close to the situation, you never notice change on a minute-by-minute basis whereas someone can see what is happening over several weeks. She also met her friend G here who had been a senior OT and had had a lot of experience getting people to walk after accidents/strokes, etc. so it was useful to get a second opinion. The time flew by. We went to see Mavis, then Helen, then Mavis, had a cup of coffee, went back to see Helen, then back to Mavis and eventually we went home. Heather and I drove down to the pub for Sunday lunch and we had a good talk. She confirmed what the Professor had indicated earlier: The recovery of patients within the first two to three weeks was indicative of how much of an eventual recovery could be expected. She was not at all hopeful, as G had confirmed what everyone else seemed to be saying: Mavis would never walk again and it was difficult to imagine much further improvement. She was also worried that Mavis did not seem to be actively responding to people but was always very passive. We went back to the ward after lunch and Mavis was desperately trying to stay awake. Just as we were leaving, I think in response to Heather's earlier point, I said to Mavis that if she doesn't start to work harder at getting better she will end up in a Nursing Home and that would be unfair on both of us. Heather returned to Derby on Sunday afternoon. It was super to have seen her and to have her support. My evenings returned to the surrounding love and company of Bill and Pat. Supper was always supplied and it did not matter if I knocked on the door at 22:00 or midnight there was always a welcome. Polly and Ed part of the clan of friends I spoke of earlier, rang for progress and said they would be coming to see Mavis in the week, so it was something both Mavis and I could look forward to.

Monday 12th July 2004.

It was that "for all of you watching in black and white the ball behind the green is the blue one", syndrome. I had developed, over the days, a way of asking questions to try to solicit the correct response. "Are you still constipated" "Yes" "Do you want your glasses on?" "No", "Has anyone been to see you today?" "Yes" "A Doctor?" "Yes," "What did he say?" Silence! Still three Yeses and one No in a row were good. It was becoming clear that if Mavis was going to start to recover she needed a lot of help and I confess to being very dubious about what help she was getting in the hospital. In fact, as far as I could see it was very little, if any. As I said earlier, things like this change both your perspective and your priorities and right now Mavis was number one priority. As I was spending more hours in the hospital per week than a junior doctor, it seemed natural to become involved. Since the physio and ward rounds during the week were usually in the morning, afternoons became lesson time.

As Mavis's face was still partially paralysed down the left side, it made understanding her when she did speak very difficult. We decided therefore that face exercises would be the best thing to start with. With concentrated effort, I transformed myself into Dr. Doolittle straight from My Fair Lady. A..., E..., I..., O..., U..., "and repeat again, and again, now try to say it backwards". Very basic, but that was all Mavis could manage and only for a very short time. To try to intersperse the boredom with something more interesting we also tried to tell the time. I could not remember how Mavis had taught the children when they were young so we started with the O'clocks, then to the half hours and then to the ¼ hours and so on. It would take over a month, but eventually Mavis asked if she could have her watch on so that she knew what the time was. Since Mavis was admitted, the ward clock had never worked.

Yet another appointment to see the Doctor about Mavis's constipation. I think by now my imagination was beginning to take over. The cartoons of people exploding came to mind with the inevitable consequences, but at least the ward would have to be cleaned properly afterwards (perhaps). I think they were all getting concerned that bowels were not moving so a meeting between three doctors and the ward manager was convened around the bedside. A plan was formed and action taken. It involved pills and tablets being inserted in all the usual places together with liquid medicine and other stuff taken orally. We wait with anticipation!

Tuesday 13th July 2004.
Mavis's physio has decided that today they will try to get Mavis to

stand upright on her own and so she is again pushed in the big Blue chair to the physio room. There is always a time in life isn't there, when you want things to happen but not at that precise moment. All of us are hoping that the constipation remedies do not kick in too quickly. With a physio on each side, Mavis is lifted to her feet. 'F', the physio was very good at telling Mavis exactly what to do, what was happening, or what was likely to happen. Unfortunately, nobody had told Mavis to breathe while she was doing this and nobody had noticed that she didn't. Just like ER or Casualty, DRAMA. Mavis collapses and poor 'F', who has only been with the hospital for four weeks, sees her first death at the hospital flash before her eyes. A cry for help results in four nurses and three doctors rushing to the physio room that could only hold about eight people maximum anyway. They all managed to squeeze in and somehow I was squeezed out. I peered between the legs and saw Mavis on the floor with 'F' checking for any vital signs. Had Mavis had another stroke, a heart attack? Mavis came round and everyone breathed a big sigh of relief. All the checks were done and Yes Mavis was still alive and yes, nobody really knew why she had collapsed in the first place. Subsequent happenings suggested that Mavis's brain just could not cope with her having to concentrate on standing and breathing at the same time.

Wednesday 14th July 2004.

About noon, Polly and Ed arrived and Mavis made a special effort to stay awake. Polly brought some photographs of our recent holiday together and Mavis looked at them with interest. Half an hour later Mavis was sound asleep. We all trouped up to Helen's ward and passed some time with her. The staff were happy that if all went well Helen should be fit to leave next week and so we keep our fingers crossed. As Polly and Ed had not seen the new city centre and 'F' the physio had said that Mavis would need clothes instead of the ward nightdress, we took the opportunity to go shopping. It was a clear warm day, most unlike Sunderland really, and we went from shop to shop looking for trendy tracksuits in a size 18. Not too many of those; so we settled for different trousers and tops and after a cup of coffee and an ice cream we returned to the ward in time to feed Mavis the evening meal. I thought that as Polly and Ed lived some 300 miles away they would have at least stopped the night, however they said they needed to get home but wanted to eat first. Where to eat? It had to be quick but pleasant so we decided to get a take away from the Indian restaurant just around the corner from the hospital and take it home to eat. Mavis was extremely tired anyway from all the excitement, so we said our farewells and left. Now I do not know if Ed had been overcome by grief at seeing how bad Mavis was or whether he just liked curry - but once we were home and we had all eaten as much as we could, I put the rest in the freezer, and it lasted me in meals for another week! Polly and Ed left at 22:00 so wouldn't be home until at least two in the morning. What great friends we have.

Thursday 15th July 2004.

I was informed as soon as I went into the ward that Mavis's bowels had moved. I didn't ask any other questions. We now started on the alphabet and managed to get to G before the sequence all went wrong. Still it was an improvement.

Friday 16th July 2004

More lessons! "What is your Name?" "Where do you live?" "What are our grandchildren called?" "Who is Ailsa married to?" "Who is Heather married to?" I had to be very selective in what questions I asked and the way I asked them, as the answers (or lack of them) could have been down to two reasons. Either Mavis genuinely did not know the answer because it had been wiped from her memory or, it was because of a conditions called Dysphasia. This is where the person knows the answer but because of the gaps left in the various parts of the brain they cannot express it. For instance, they may know how old they are but if you asked them, they would not be able to tell you.

During the lessons, a minister came round the ward and stopped to talk. He was the hospital chaplain and invited Mavis to the Sunday service. I told him she would love to go but I cannot get her there as the ward does not have a wheelchair and the big blue chair is not practical entering and exiting the lifts, as it has such small castors. "Not a problem" he replied, "just come to the chapel about half an hour before the service starts and collect one of ours." Wow, Mavis for the first time in nearly five weeks can go out of the prison. Sorry, I mean ward.

Faith is the Anchor.

I have been able to write this book because Mavis was allowed to live. Had she died, there would not have been not a lot to write about and no doubt my life would have been considerably different. So, has our faith been tested? No, I don't think so, as our faith was very strong beforehand. However, it has been deepened. Faith only becomes faith when there is nothing left to hold on to and there were times when only God could comfort me. The real acceptance of this for me was when I was on the telephone to the Rev. John Boyers. (page 9) I had already accepted that God's will was going to be done, but when John asked if he could pray with me and I asked him what we were going to pray for his reply of "That God's will be done" somehow gave me great comfort. Had the outcome been different would I have still felt the same? I would like to think so but who knows. There are many people that have gone through similar or worse circumstances without faith and still survive well. For me however I believe that the strength I got to continue when all else seemed to be falling away around me, came from our Jesus who accepts me as I am and asks only one thing of me in return, that I believe in him. God did not make this happen although I believe he may allowed it to, Job in the bible is a good example of how God sometimes lets things happen. However I believe that when we become Christians we invite God into our life and therefore take him with us. It does not make us immune from life's troubles but he does promise to be there with us to help us through them. After all, if becoming a Christian made us immune then everyone would want to join the club so to speak and many would miss out on the very personal one to one relationship true Christians have with Christ. I have not met anyone yet that having had a true experience of God has said that they have regretted it.

Chapter 5
The Recovery Starts.

Saturday 17th July 2004.

Margaret and Keith arrived for another visit and stopped long enough to see Mavis have her evening meal. Remembering that Mavis was still on slops, despite me asking several times for these to be cancelled, it was hardly surprising that Mavis was beginning to lose interest in food. Feeding her ourselves was the only way to ensure she would eat something and ice cream had become one of her favourites. Now, since Mavis could do very little for herself, it still sticks in our memory that on this Saturday we were all talking and not taking much notice of her. Within what seemed a nano second Mavis had devoured one ice cream and was asking for another. If a way to a man is through his stomach then perhaps ice cream was going to be the way to Mavis's brain! We asked the nurse if she could have another and one was duly produced which again was devoured in seconds. Perhaps a third was being greedy but who cares? It is about time Mavis had something she liked and if she could eat it on her own so much the better.

Sunday 18th July 2004.

After lunch, I informed the staff that I was going to take Mavis off ward and down to church for the first time. I would need them to hoist her from the big blue chair into the wheelchair I was to pick up from the chaplaincy. At about 14:45 I bounded down to the chapel to get a wheelchair but when I arrived, it was empty. This could not be happening! Everyone on the ward was all geared up for Mavis to go to chapel and I could not even play my part and find the wheelchair. I sat in total despair for what seemed an eternity when I heard movements from behind a screen, there appeared a man with not one but two wheelchairs, and yes, one of those was for us. I raced back to the ward, in due course Mavis was hoisted into it, and we set off for the chapel. When we arrived there Mavis cried, and cried. What had I done now? I was now beginning to realise that one of the main problems of the stroke was that it had rearranged her organs and somehow her bladder had been moved very much closer to her eyeballs, as every time something happened she cried. My problem was that being a mere male, I could seldom tell why she cried. Were they tears of joy, tears of sadness, tears of helplessness, or just self-pity? It was going to take me a long time to find out. She cried most of the way through the service. I would love to tell you why but I cannot. She tells me now it was a mixture of all emotions and I have to accept that. After the service, the sun was shining so instead of going straight back to the ward we ventured out into the hospital grounds. If you picture these as tranquil gardens, with a soft waterfall or fountain, forget it. We walked from one building to another and around the car parks. Outside for the first time since having her stroke it must have seemed very strange. The only thing Mavis could say was that it was very good to be alive.

Monday 19th July 2004.

The ward looked different today. The beds were made and everything was spick and span. Enquiring from one of the cleaners, I was told that everyone has had to make a special effort, as it was Matron's visit this afternoon. We waited in anticipation to see what Matron was like. The Hattie Jacques image from Carry On Nursing could not have been further from the truth. A small demure lady in a crisp white overall arrived in the afternoon. After spending some time with the nursing staff, she was escorted round the ward to meet individual patients. She took the time to come and talk to Mavis and me catching me off guard when she said she would like to have a meeting with me on my own later. I don't know whether I had been labelled as a troublemaker or not, but why was I being singled out? Matron could not have been nicer. She apologised that Mavis's experience had been so distasteful during her stay and assured me that she would try to make sure that all the complaints I had raised so far would be investigated properly and she would keep an eye on things. She mentioned that we had not seen her earlier as she had been on holiday in Germany. It later transpired that her husband had been seriously ill while working in Germany and she had been at his bedside for the last four weeks.

When I asked if it would be possible for Mavis to have a proper bath, it was obvious from her response that Mavis should have been having proper baths already but to date bed baths were all that had happened. I also remarked that if the ward had a wheelchair then maybe the physio, and for that matter the nursing staff, would find it a lot easier to push patients round instead of the big blue vinyl armchair that Mavis had almost claimed as her own! It was talking about the wheelchair that sparked a thought in my mind, you know the one that sort of creeps in and before you know it, takes over everything. If the chapel had a wheelchair they might use it only on Sundays to take people to church so, what was it being used for the rest of the time? The meeting with Matron concluded and before returning to Mavis, it was a quick nip into the chapel. "Hello Rev., can I borrow your wheelchair?" We discussed the ins and outs and Yes, I would not nick it and Yes, I would take good care of it, and, Yes, I could borrow it if it was free. And Yes again. Remarkably, it would be free this afternoon. A result!

I remember it well. It was hot with a few heavy clouds but this afternoon Mavis and I were going to have an adventure. Having checked that the wheelchair was still free I went up to the ward and begged the nurses to hoist Mavis into it. So the journey began. With the urine bag tied to the leg fairly high up so it was not visible we marched out of the hospital grounds. Wasn't this super, freedom at last. To the novices amongst you I offer a tip. When making a plan make sure you have a follow up of what to do next. Having got out of the hospital where were we going to go? Now Barbara and Alan, some very dear friends of ours for many years, lived only about five minutes car ride away from the hospital. How about going there? We would not be able to go in but at least we could talk to them for a few minutes. It is amazing how quickly a car travels in five minutes isn't it? When you are pushing a wheelchair with nearly 15st in it up a hill it seemed an awful long way, but it was something to aim for.

We rounded the first bend. I looked at Mavis and asked if she was enjoying herself. Through the tears, I got a Yes or at least I thought it was but then a nod confirmed and we progressed further. Seconds later

I heard an ow! ow! Ow! Ow! Moreover, the wheelchair was suddenly a lot more difficult to push. I stopped and asked Mavis what was wrong. She could not speak because of the pain. She pointed to her left foot that had become detached from the footrest. This was now trapped under the footrest. Ummm nobody had told me that this might happen but on the other hand, I suppose I had not told them I was going to take Mavis out. They probably thought it was for just short internal journeys within the hospital. Now the thinking really had to start. I could not lift Mavis up to raise the chair as her foot was stuck underneath it. I could not slide the foot out because of the way it was stuck and I could not take the wheelchair back as it would have caused too much pain and possibly broken her ankle. The only way was to lift the wheelchair from the back but to do this meant I could not then move the foot to put it in a safe position. Fortunately for us the Lord had already seen our predicament and had sent help by way of two paramedics who had just come out of the sandwich shop. As I lifted up the chair one of them secured Mavis's foot and put it back on the footplate. Yes, it was sore but no damage done.

We progressed on our way with Mavis under strict instructions to shout, "Foot" if she felt it was coming off again so to speak. With a shout of "foot" about every 100 yards, progress was slow but eventually 1 hour 25 minutes later we arrived at Barbara and Alan's house. I just hoped they were in! We waited in anxious anticipation after the doorbell was rung. Yes, they were in and as they came to the door great feelings were exchanged; theirs of welcome and genuine joy to see us and mine of relief and thank goodness I had made it! I knew that I could never get the wheelchair inside their house, as the steps were too many and too steep, so in best English tradition we decided to have a tea party on the drive. Picnic chairs and table were summoned from the garage and tea and biscuits were produced as suitable and much needed refreshment. During the conversation, Barbara offered to come to the hospital in the late afternoons to a) visit Mavis but b) to make sure she was eating her food properly. This was very gratefully accepted as I knew it would not be long before Helen would be discharged from hospital, and it meant that I could spend more time at home in the afternoon. We passed a very enjoyable afternoon and bade our farewells at just after 5 o'clock giving me 45 minutes to get back to the ward for the evening meal. Going downhill with someone in a wheelchair is infinitely easier than pushing them up hill and apart from 'foot' stops every 100 yards or so, we were back on the ward in time for tea without anyone knowing of our first real adventure.

Tuesday 20th July 2004.

I asked the staff if Mavis could have a bath again and was told, "If we can find the time", but nothing happened. Meanwhile, we keep going through the alphabet and progress has been good. Mavis can now count up to 50 and can recite the alphabet through from A - Z in about 5 minutes with a lot of concentration and many mistakes. She can now remember her Christian name, Surname and some of her address, but postcode and telephone numbers just don't stand a chance. Physiotherapy continues on the ward but without much improvement. Dinnertime comes and the nurses are going around asking what people would like to eat. As usual, Mavis is not interested in the liquid food and nothing of the slop variety appeals. They disappeared to the far end of the Ward and another nurse asked Mavis again what she would like to eat. We looked at each other and I can see the look of "just give me something nice" on her face so I asked them if they have any pies. They have and so Mavis settles down to pie, peas, and potatoes. At last something solid. She accomplishes it all admirably and thinks that from now on she will be able to have solid food again. Unfortunately, the staff nurse found out and we are told off as Mavis might have "choked on real food", but we are told that the speech therapist returns on Monday and Mavis will be on her list.

Thursday 22nd July 2004.

True to his word Dr. M, the consultant from Monkwearmouth hospital, arrived and reassessed Mavis. Now whether it was Mavis's hard work over the last two weeks, or it was because Mavis still hadn't had a bath and was beginning to get a little bit whiffy, or even that the ward wanted rid of both of us I don't know; but this time he thought she could be transferred to the rehab ward in Monkwearmouth Hospital and it would happen as soon as a bed became available.

Friday 23rd July 2004.

Matron popped in for a visit while Mavis and I are having our lessons and I asked her about Mavis going back on to solid food. She explained that she couldn't do that until Mavis had been seen again by the speech therapist and she has been away on holiday. So as soon as she returns... Mavis and I go back to our lessons. Telling the time is now usually good with only the odd mistake but whether it means anything I am beginning to doubt and I realise what a difficult concept time really is. It is only really useful when living in a demanding world. Cocooned in a world where everything is done for you and there is little interactivity, it really has little relevance. No wonder children find it difficult.

It was Margaret's birthday/retirement party this weekend and we were supposed to be had been going. Dilemma. Do we not go at all or do I go on my own. I even thought about the possibility of taking Mavis but I would never get her into or out of the car let alone dressed. It would be all right if she just wanted to pass urine, as she was still catheterised, but what if she wanted to move her bowels? No! Was the resounding result of a two-minute debate in my head. I discussed it at length with Mavis and others and eventually decided it was probably better to go on my own. I took the video recorder into the ward and filmed Mavis trying to make a speech, the sort of thing you see on "This is your life". We rehearsed the few words Mavis could remember time and time again and eventually got enough on tape to make it sound reasonable.

Saturday 24th July 2004.

I said farewell to Mavis and felt terribly guilty about it. As I drove onto the dual carriageway, I had to fight a very strong feeling not to turn back but eventually I arrived in Bridlington. I changed at their house and then we all set off for what was going to be a very big surprise for Margaret. Keith had arranged a big party with all the gang invited together with many of Margaret's friends and colleagues, and Margaret had thought we were just going out for dinner together. During the evening I was very well looked after and I would never complain but it was just the odd things that start to bring home to you what it might have been like if Mavis had died. The restaurant had still set the table for the correct number of place settings so that when I sat down there was an empty one next to me. Ouch, it hurt! Mavis and I had always loved dancing so it hurt again that she was not there to dance with. The rest of the gang made me dance with them, which was nice, and eventually I got through the evening but gosh, even with all those people there, it wasn't half-lonely! Despite the late hour all the gang went back to Margaret and Keith's as they all wanted to see the video. As the only video machine working at the time was up in their bedroom we all congregated on their bed and eleven of us watched 2 minutes and 45 seconds of Mavis wishing Margaret a very happy birthday. Not a dry eye in the house!

Monday 26th July 2004.

Sure enough at about 11:30 the Speech Therapist arrived. Now for some reason I expected this session to be a very scientific evaluation of whether Mavis could swallow or not. Perhaps it was, and I misjudged it, but it consisted of the woman going to the fridge and extracting a freshly made sandwich. This she gave to Mavis to eat and after Mavis had eaten it, she took down the "soft food only" sign and Mavis could now officially eat proper food! Having just eaten a large sandwich the staff now came around giving out lunch and wondered why Mavis was not feeling hungry. With little happening on the physio front, I thought it might be useful if we tried to do some ourselves. I asked a nurse if she could find me a belt or bandage so that I could tie Mavis's legs together. She says she cannot so I have to improvise with the belt off my trousers. My logic is that if I tied the good leg to the bad, then Mavis can use the good one to move the bad one. This at least will tell the muscles in both legs that they have to do some work. I get some very disapproving looks from the general medical team but nobody attempted to stop me.

Tuesday 27th July 2004.

I visited Helen first this morning, and I was told that she would definitely be coming home this week. Mixed feelings but I would cope. I went down to see Mavis and what a transformation. She has had a proper bath, they had washed her hair, and a couple of the nurses had combed and brushed it for her. She positively beamed. Welcome back into the real world Mavis. Now say after me A..., E..., I..., O..., U.

Thursday 29th July 2004.

I went to Helen's ward to make sure that she is coming home today and I am greeted by Helen dressed and waiting. She knows she is going home but she cannot understand why she has to "leave this nice hotel where the servants are so friendly and helpful". I went down, visited Mavis for a while, and then back up to Helen. She is still waiting for the pharmacist to supply the medicines she needs when she goes home, so back down to re visit Mavis for the afternoon lessons. A little set back as today after about six attempts we only get to the letter 'M.' However she can almost tell the time again, but still just gets a little confused on 'past' and 'to'. I cannot decide whether she knows what it should be and the words just come out wrong or whether she genuinely does not know, but overall it is still progress. Returning to Helen's ward, I am told that Helen cannot come home now because the occupational therapist is on holiday. Helen will not be seen for another week.

This strikes me as crazy. There is no medical reason why Helen should be in hospital and surely, they need the beds. I get confirmation about Helen's medical state and tell the staff that as soon as Helen's medicine arrives I am taking her home. If the occupational therapist wants to see her, they can come to the house. Bolshy or what! I managed to obtain a wheelchair for Helen and I went to get the car, parked it outside, and then went to fetch Helen. I wheeled her down to the car and put her in. She is so frail, all skin and bone. I wondered if she has been fed on the ward but I cannot see to both patients and I assumed that as the "servants" had been good to her while she was in there, I attributed the weight loss to just one of those things that happened to old people when they are in hospital. I then had to return the wheelchair and felt guilty that my car was parked where it should not be, but hey, they would just have to wait. Why can't hospitals have a loading and unloading zone say by a back entrance where you can take and collect patients, particularly the elderly and/or infirm, when they are not going by ambulance,?

We both returned home and I cooked dinner for Helen. Certainly nothing wrong with her appetite. I took her to her bedroom so she can watch her television, but she could not remember how to operate it. Back to more lessons... and I never wanted to be a teacher!

The weekend passed well. Helen seemed to be settled, and apart from the odd bit of confusion seemed unaffected by me looking after her; but I would say that wouldn't I?

Monday 2nd August 2004.

Matron came to tell us the good news and the not so good news. A bed would become available at Monkwearmouth hospital this week and Mavis will be moved on Friday. Hurray! The not so good news was that they still could not find a harness for the hoist so still no bath, but Matron is still on the case! On returning home I find a message on the answer phone from Helen's occupational therapist saying that she is coming to evaluate Helen's situation on Wednesday.

Wednesday 4th August 2004.

After visiting Mavis I returned home explaining before I left that I would not be back in the afternoon as I was expecting a visit from Helen's hospital OT.

She arrived and was not very pleasant. I got the distinct feeling that I should not have brought Helen home without her seeing Helen first, but if people will go on holiday what else do they expect? The inspection went well and I mentioned to her that Helen's granddaughter is an OT, so we did know what we were doing. The attitude softened a bit now, so we settled to having a general conversation about how I am going to cope with Helen's wellbeing. She seemed reasonably satisfied and when about to leave asked if there was anything else I thought I needed. I remarked that a wheelchair for Helen might be very useful for taking her both to church and to her various hospital appointments. I think it was said more in ironic enthusiasm rather than genuine belief that Helen might actually receive one, especially after all the problems of trying to get Mavis a wheelchair at the hospital. Now I do not know whether it was the fact that I had mentioned that Heather was an OT earlier that had any effect or not, but to my utter disbelief Helen's OT said one would be arranged and to expect it within a couple of weeks. Seeing is believing, I thought, and went back to the hospital to let Mavis know what had transpired.

Thursday 5th August 2004.

Rumour has it amongst the nursing staff that Mavis might not go to Monkwearmouth on Friday as the ward is closed due to an infectious outbreak, but we cannot get clarification so everything is still geared to moving on Friday.

Friday 6th August 2004.

I arrived at the hospital early as the ambulance was booked to collect Mavis for about 11:00. At about 10:15 matron arrived on the ward and after discussions with the ward staff came over to tell us that due to an infectious outbreak on the ward Mavis should have been going to it will not now happen. Assurances were given that as soon as things clear up Mavis will be moved, possibly as soon as Monday but no promises. At 11.00 the ambulance men turned up as nobody had told them that Mavis was not going today, which upsets Mavis even more.

For the next seven days, we seemed to live in limbo land. I tried to take our minds off things by 'borrowing' the wheelchair from the chapel and going 'off ward' whenever we could. I overcame the problem of Mavis's left leg keep falling off the wheelchair by taking a strap with me and tying it to her right leg. I am feeling fitter by the day with all the exercise but somehow the move to Monkwearmouth seems to get further and further away. We spend the time repeatedly attempting to tell the time, reciting the alphabet, and building the family tree mentally. Mavis can now remember who the children are and who I am but, remembering the names of the grandchildren and to whom they belong, is proving a lot more difficult. I also try to do some physiotherapy with her myself which the nursing staff tell me off about. Perhaps it was because they saw me tying the left leg to the right one again and getting Mavis to exercise both legs together that they thought it was not exactly scientific.

Helen is coping at home very well. Providing I arrive for meal times and she is fed, she seems happy watching the television all day. She used to read avidly but I think the last stroke took away her ability to understand what she was reading and her concentration levels had been diminished to the point that even when she did read, she told me she could not remember it. I really felt so sorry for her; if Mavis had not had the stroke then she would still be at home able to look after Helen. As it was, Helen just has to have her own company, at least until I manage to get everything sorted out.

Tuesday 10th August 2004.

I awake to a telephone call at 8:30 from the NHS delivery man and to my total disbelief and admiration, just after nine a brand new shiny wheelchair is delivered. If the NHS can be this efficient in some departments outside the hospital, why can't they be a little better inside? I go to the hospital and assail Matron again. As Mavis is leaving the ward, I do not mind treading on a few toes a little harder to try to organise a bath for Mavis. Even perhaps, the use of a wheelchair inside the ward instead of the big blue chair, which next to her bed, is still Mavis's official residency. Matron cannot do anything about the wheelchair but she will find out about why Mavis has not had a bath. After about half an hour she comes to tell us that the reason Mavis has not had a bath is that they need a harness to lift Mavis with the hoist into the bath and it has gone missing. Supposedly, it had been sent to the laundry service and had never come back. This despite the fact that it is bright yellow with ward D41 printed all over it. She had despatched someone to the laundry to see if anyone could locate it and if not she would try to borrow one from another ward. This really brings home the point that it is not that the NHS does not have any money; it is more the fact that a very high percentage of the money and time they do have is being wasted!

It is a very nice day again today so I nip down to see the chaplain and ask if I can borrow their wheelchair again this afternoon. Wonderful, and with a promise to take great care and not to trap the foot this time I push Mavis up to the nearest park. Well, it is not so much a park really as a cemetery, but the air is fresh away from the main roads and the flowers are looking and smelling good so it is good to be alive no matter where you are. Somehow, the graves offer a stark reminder how fragile life really is and how close to the edge some of us get sometimes.

Wednesday 11th August 2004.

A triumph over inefficiency! A harness has been located and Mavis can have her second proper bath since being admitted to hospital on June 15th. Now fresh and feeling so much cleaner the lessons in the afternoon go well. We work through numbers, the alphabet backwards, and the time with few mistakes. The home address is good providing you do not have to have the postcode, but the telephone number is still just a range of random digits.

Thursday 12th August 2004

After anticipating news of the move every day, eventually it arrived today. Subject to the ward staying clear of infection, the move was on for tomorrow morning. Wow time to go at last! "Now Mavis, remember to say goodbye to all the staff that you won't be seeing tomorrow!"

Obstacles not mountains.

For every action, there is an equal and opposite reaction, or so they tell me. My reaction to incompetence, including my own, is usually frustration leading to anger. As I have got older, I have learnt to realise that one persons mountain is to another a mere obstacle that simply needs to be removed. I can highlight this by way of a short illustration. Just before Mavis had her stroke the 'gang' of us were together in the Lake district and it was a lovely day. We were trying to decide what to do for the day and eventually it was agreed that the women would go shopping and the men walking. We knew two of the men with us were strong walkers but as they had promised to be careful with us we departed on what was going to be a casual walk through the hills. After we had been climbing for what seemed hours and the oxygen had become so very thin we could hardly take more than two steps at a time, three of us were feeling very much the worst for wear. Summoning every last bit of energy to continue to the top we watched in complete admiration as a fell runner came past us at a great speed showing little or no signs of effort. To us we were climbing the mountain, to him it was just a little obstacle to overcome to get to where he needed to go to. My mountain was trying not to get angry every time something went wrong as they often did. By trying to stay calm they simply became obstacles that needed removing. Shouting at the nurses didn't help me get the desired effect as they neither had the authority or the power to change things and so became my mountain. Asking politely but firmly to try to get obstacles moved did have a greater beneficial result. So when the cutlery is dirty, when the same question is asked over and over again, when your loved one doesn't appear to be getting the treatment you think they deserve, remember you can help remove obstacles but mountains need an awful lot more effort.

Chapter 6
Another Day Another Venue.

Friday 13th August 2004.

10:30 and everyone is geared to move Mavis to the new hospital, all we need now is the ambulance. At about 11:30 it arrived and with a great relief, Mavis was stretchered out of D41 and onto a completely new experience.

The two hospitals are not very far apart but there were two people going, Mavis and another gentleman from the ward. It seemed to take forever to get there. I had decided to go by car as it would be easier to get home that way and I arrived at the hospital well before the ambulance. I waited and eventually it arrived. The gentleman was in a wheelchair and Mavis was strapped into the bed/stretcher so they took the man in first. When I looked at Mavis she was sobbing her heart out, but I was sure it was not because she had left the other hospital. Having now met many stroke survivors, the one thing they all suffer from is fear of the unknown brought about by a complete loss of confidence either in themselves or in others. This was the first time Mavis had been outside the hospital without me, and consuming fear and panic had taken over. I tried to reassure her and in so doing mistakenly gave her my hand to hold. This was seized in such an amazing grip that I then had to escort Mavis on the stretcher from the ambulance to the ward with my fingers turning whiter by the minute.

We arrived on the ward bay, which had three beds. It was bright, cheerful, and above all clean. The Ward sister came and introduced herself and the staff to us, then immediately set about making Mavis comfortable. Ailsa arrived and she was asked if she and I could go and see the Sister when we are free. Mavis is offered lunch even though lunchtime is passed and she is given a general inspection so the staff are up to date on any problems. While Mavis eats her lunch, we go to Sister's office where she informs us exactly what they will do for Mavis and how it will be done. It seems a little perfunctory and cold and I wondered if she was always like this or she was just having an off day. We returned to Mavis and started talking to a nurse who is doing various checks on Mavis and she asks us a few questions. Some we can answer but some we cannot and therefore she has to go and find Mavis's file. As she opens the file, I noticed that tucked inside the front cover is my letter of complaint given to the D41 ward on day 16 of Mavis's admittance. No wonder the Sister's demeanour was a bit distant. Reading that in isolation, she must have thought that all we did was to complain. I went and found Sister and asked if I could have another talk with her. She was extremely wary until I explained the reasons behind my complaints, then she looked a little shocked. She warmed immediately, and told me they would do everything they could to make sure Mavis did not suffer in anyway, and that her time in the ward should be as enjoyable as possible, although it was not going to be any picnic.

Feeling happier now both sides understood the situation, we returned to the ward where the nurse asked us if we knew of any reason why Mavis still had a catheter in. I was tempted to say 'because the nursing staff at the previous hospital were too idle to toilet her' but not wishing to possibly sour the existing fragile relationship I just said we didn't know and within 30 minutes it had been removed. Mavis had suffered pain and discomfort from the catheter for some weeks now, and to have it removed was a tremendous relief. She was worried that she would wet the bed, so the nursing staff spent a long time with her assuring that if she needed the toilet, she just had to ring the buzzer and someone would come; and quickly. They had just left when Mavis felt she needed to go, so we put it to the test, and Yes, they did come quickly, and Yes, they were attentive, and Yes, things were so completely different and improved it was hard to believe it belonged to the same hospital trust.

Saturday 14th August 2004.

I arrived on the ward at the usual time to feed Mavis, and shock horror she was not there. Now I know I just said that stroke people suffer from a total lack of confidence afterwards but I have to admit that after our experience of D41 I was not exactly confident myself. Had the move been too much for her? Had she had another stroke? Where was she? The layout of the ward was still new to me so I went to the nursing station and I was told that Mavis was having her breakfast in the dining room. I could hardly answer with surprise but lo and behold there was Mavis in a wheel chair sitting at a table with others eating breakfast. Fantastic! Not only was she eating breakfast but afterwards she was going to have a bath! Two things in one day, what joy!

Feeling that now she was in capable hands, I left, returning to look after Helen, promising to come back in the afternoon, probably after lunch. When I did, again Mavis was missing. Where was she this time? Eventually I found her sitting in the dining room, which in between meals doubled as a resident's lounge. There were a few people there and Mavis already seemed to have a visitor. The lady was smartly dressed and I assumed she was a hospital visitor of some sort. I was introduced to her, she to me as 'S' and the three of us had a usual type of conversation covering everything from the weather to the hospital, and everything was as normal as you could ask. Mavis was happy and seemed contented for the first time since the stroke; things were looking up.

Sunday 15th August 2004.

As Mavis seemed to be well looked after now, I took the opportunity of taking Helen to church. She was received with great warmth and everyone made a fuss of her. It was funny to see her, proud as punch, showing everyone her brand new wheelchair. Three months ago if you had suggested she even got into a wheelchair to go shopping you would have been met with a very vehement No! Now it seemed to have become a status symbol, like a teenager with an ASBO. This afternoon I went to see Mavis and was a little surprised to see 'S' there again but this time after a short conversation she left and I assumed she had gone to visit somebody else. Remarking on this to Mavis I was shocked when she told me that no, 'S' was not a visitor but a patient. She had had her stroke about two months before Mavis and although her body had made a complete physical recovery, the stroke had removed all of her memory. She could not go home as her husband worked away but she was not really ill enough to stay in hospital and the staff were desperately trying to find somewhere for her to live. Thank goodness I thought; although

Mavis was still physically incapacitated, she did seem to have a little memory and it was improving.

It was a nice day and I asked if Mavis could leave the hospital ward. The staff looked amazed. All I had to do, in the future, was make sure it did not clash with anything such as physio or any of the other activities and just ask a member of staff who would get Mavis prepared. It was so difficult to come to terms with such a wonderfully changed attitude. Mavis had her own wheelchair and all we had to do was ask so that Mavis could be hoisted from the bed to the wheelchair. How great was that! Just across from the hospital was a park, this time a proper one. We walked out in the Sunday afternoon sunshine and somehow everything seemed right with the world. Even if Mavis did not improve any more, I felt sure I could cope. We had seen how bad it could have been, so life was good again.

Monday 16th August 2004.

What a lazy start to the day knowing I did not have to arrive there until after breakfast. The other lady who had been in the ward bay with Mavis had been taken back to the other hospital, because she had become very ill, so Mavis had the ward bay to herself. Now whether this influenced the ward round or not it is hard for me to say but instead of being asked to leave this time, I was actively encouraged to stay. Dr. M gave Mavis a full medical and particularly examined Mavis's left leg and foot that had become very swollen. After the Doctor had left, the staff handed us this piece of paper that had 'timetable' written on it. This listed everything that was going to happen to Mavis through the week including Physiotherapy, Occupational Therapy, Team assessments, Speech Therapy etc. Every day was full and I wondered how Mavis was going to cope. It was going to be like running a marathon after sitting around for the last 10 weeks. Still, it had to be good for her, and the first physio session was this afternoon. The physios arrived on the ward and said they had come to collect Mavis. Staff hoisted her into the wheelchair and off she went.

I was quite happy sitting in the ward reading the many cards from the various friends and visitors when one of the physios came back and asked me why I was not going as well. They explained to me that from now on this was going to be a team effort to try to realise as much potential as Mavis could manage. This meant I was to be part of the team as well. Fantastic. To be included instead of excluded, to be expected to participate instead of being treated as if you were in the way all the time. However, it started to dawn on me that being able to participate also means having to take on some of the responsibility. Help! At the gym, they lifted Mavis from her chair onto an adjustable bench to assess what she can or cannot do. One of the first results was that they think that with some training, the staff and I can transfer Mavis from one thing to another without the need of a hoist all the time.

Now, I am not sure whether I have mentioned this before or not but Mavis is no size 0. Over our married life, she has ranged from a size 14 to a size 22 and everything in between. The last stay in hospital with no exercise and three meals a day, when Barbara and I were there to feed her, meant that she was erring on the heavier side. Thank goodness I had built up my muscles pushing the wheelchair around! They showed me how to grasp Mavis and we try it... boy was she heavy, but we made it and so it was to be for the rest of the week, up, down, up, down, up until they all felt we were beginning to conquer it.

As it was Mavis's first week it was really all assessment and it was explained to us that at the earliest opportunity, when all the tests had been done, a family meeting would occur. Here members of all the disciplines including the nursing staff meet the family to discuss results and possible prognosis. A date was fixed for 2 weeks time. Until then it was going to be full steam ahead with all the disciplines wanting their bit of the action. Now I do not know who trains these people but why do they all ask the same stupid question? It is always 'how are you'? Which is fair enough but then ask, "What is it you would like to achieve?" This question got so monotonous that before long I had prompted Mavis to answer "No.28 in the Karma Sutra," which started to take them by surprise a little, especially as we could not do it before she had her stroke (whatever it is). Mavis and I just wanted to return to normal, to get our lives back to being as close to how it was pre stroke as possible, so why ask such a stupid question?

Another major problem encountered was that if Mavis was going to attend the gym regularly she needed to have something on her feet and they could not be little fluffy slippers. The stroke had left Mavis with one foot swollen to the extent that there were three shoe sizes between her left and right foot and therefore none of her existing shoes were suitable. Fortunately, I take a similar size shoe but because I have a very high instep, it usually requires me to have a wide fitting and a slightly larger size. After trying on all her old shoes and giving up, we eventually tried on a pair of my trainers and after a fashion they fitted, so another problem solved.

Tuesday 17th August 2004.

Today we meet the speech therapist for the first time. A nice woman who spoke like every speech therapist does. Every word had to be thought about before it was delivered and therefore the appointment seemed to go on forever, but she says she will be coming back later in the week with all sorts of crosswords and puzzles, that Mavis will be able to do. Now she has done her assessment the family meeting is more likely to go ahead as planned.

Wednesday 18th August 2004.

Mavis and I go to physio and are introduced to the standing frame. This is a piece of apparatus that, as the name suggests, consists of a frame that you stand in. Your legs then are strapped into it so that you cannot move or fall over. The idea is that the left leg has some weight put on it and hopefully, the brain will start to recognise it is there. I had already read the story of a man who had had a serious stroke and after his wife had left after visiting hours, he called the nurse over and pointing to his arm, he suggested to her that his wife had left it behind. Now, whilst Mavis was not quite reduced to that state I could see the logic of it. For the standing frame to help the brain in its recognition you have to be standing in it for at least 20 minutes. As the physios hoist Mavis into it, twenty seconds seems to be nearer what she can accomplish. Still, it is a start and something to be built on.

Saturday 21st August 2004.

Margaret and Keith said they were coming to visit Mavis in her new abode today, so it seemed a good idea to do something a little different. I asked the staff if I could take Mavis out for a meal and they thought it was a great idea and they would adjust her food intake during the day accordingly. About twenty minutes walk from the hospital were a few shops that also included a Chinese and an Italian restaurant. I opted for the Italian and checked to make sure that we could get the wheelchair in. I booked the table and felt quite excited. Margaret and Keith arrived in the afternoon and went straight to the hospital to see Mavis. I stayed and looked after Helen and then in the early evening fed her and made sure she could get into bed by herself. We then left for the hospital to tell Mavis that she was going out for the evening.

It was a lovely night not cold and above all not raining. Mavis was wrapped up warmly in her own clothes plus a blanket and off we set. I do not know what I expected; I suppose I thought it would be like any other time we had gone out for a meal only this time Mavis would simply be in a wheelchair. How wrong can you be? We settled at the table and the waiter gave Mavis the menu. As she looked at it, tears began to come and I tried to find out what was the matter this time. In between sobs, she explained that the noise from all the other people in the restaurant was hurting her brain and she was unable to cope with the menu. This was the first time I think any of us had realised how much the stroke had affected Mavis's ability to cope with everyday things that we all accept as normal. I asked why she could not cope with the menu and she explained that as soon as she read one line and started on the second she could not retain what she had read. So in fact, her choice from the menu could only be the last thing that she had read. She knew this was wrong but could do nothing about it, so I selected something I knew she liked and we had a great meal. The other thing I thought a little strange was that she did not want anything to drink. She thought that if she did not drink anything then she would not have to go to the loo, which she knew she could not manage, so not all the reasoning of the brain has been lost.

About 21:45, we arrived back at the hospital and all was locked up. We had to ring the bell for the night porter to let us in and we explained where we had been and why we were late back. He seemed as delighted as Mavis that she had been out and so we made our way back to the ward. The night staff crowded around Mavis, excited to see how she had managed and made her feel very special that she had accomplished the evening so well. We all got Mavis ready for bed and a very tired lady retired for the night completely exhausted. Although Mavis had been in somewhat difficult surroundings, she had coped very well and Keith remarked how much better she looked and that he felt she had come on in leaps and bounds as she could now talk a little bit more clearly and was making sense.

Monday 21st August 2004.

According to the timetable, Mavis had a free afternoon today so I cleared it with the staff that I would take her out, as it was a nice day. Where do I take her? Monkwearmouth hospital is situated about 1 .5 miles from the sea and as nearly anyone will tell you if you have lived close to the sea, even if you didn't visit it regularly when it was there, you miss it terribly when you can't get to it. So, off we went to the beach. It was a long walk pushing the chair and you quickly find out that not all roads have suitable crossing places, but after 40 minutes we arrived. Although you seemed to be walking on the level, logic tells you that "going DOWN to the beach" probably means just that. The tide was nearly all the way out and we have a wonderful sandy beach. We walked along the promenade for about another mile and sat to have an ice cream. I looked at Mavis and the tears are again streaming down her face. You know the paper-folding toy that children make and then they come and ask you to pick a number and then a colour and so on until it tells you that you will marry the girl next door. Well... sometimes I think I ought to carry one of those around and by thinking of various numbers, it might eventually guide me as to why Mavis keeps crying. This time it turns out to be that again, the reality of her situation has come home and she tells me through the tears that "she will never be able to go down onto the sand again", I realise that this is probably true but "hey you can see the sea and the sand, how good is that"! We finish with the tears and ice cream and I plan our route back to the hospital. By going back a different way; I can just manage the hills. They are not so steep but a lot longer. As we arrived back at the hospital I noticed just how much I have sweated and now it is my turn to smell. Still never mind, with a bit of luck people will think it's Mavis won't they?

Helen.

A little bit about Helen. When I came to stay that first Christmas she was just into her fifties. A new wife of only five years who had taken on this widower from the North East and his teenage daughter. She was Scottish being born just outside Glasgow and just after the war had emigrated to Canada. She returned to the UK about four years later to look after her mother when she became seriously ill. Although she lived in England, she was always a Scot particularly after losing her husband. Unfortunately for her, she was driving when their car hit black ice on the A74 Carlisle to Glasgow road and he was dead at the scene and she did die in hospital but was revived again. She stayed in hospital for nearly 3 months and was then released home to be looked after by Mavis. She suffered enormously from the guilt of the tragedy but slowly recovered to the point that we felt she could cope on her own after we got married in 1967. Three months after this she had a nervous breakdown and came to live with us from that time on. The children gave her a new purpose for living and she became their live in Gran while Mavis went back to work. She was an encourager and extremely generous to all the family. Christmas time was always, understandably, filled with tension because of her remembrance and you could feel it building as the season approached. To help all our sanity she used to return to Scotland to stay with friends over New Year and when she returned had taken up the accent so strongly that it took me time to start understanding her again. She became an intricate part of our family life.

Chapter 7
We break the first rule.

Saturday 28th August 2004.

After nearly two weeks of practice at transferring, we were now masters at it and it struck me, we were fast approaching the first major step. If Mavis could transfer from wheelchair to car then another completely new world would open up for us. Instead of being stuck inside all the time, we could go out, see things, and go to different places. On the previous Saturday, I had asked non-specific questions about taking Mavis out of the hospital. I was told it was encouraged for her to go out but one of the main conditions was that for some reason she could not be taken home. It seemed a strange thing to say as we lived there and the more I thought about it the more I was inclined to think it was a rule that we needed to break. I had asked Mavis on the previous Sunday what would she really like to do and she had replied to go home. I think she had meant permanently not just for a visit, as I had intended. So today was the day, we would break all the rules and attempt not to be caught with egg all over our faces.

I parked the car round the back of the hospital, where it could not be seen from the ward, and went to pick Mavis up in the wheelchair. We left with the usual gestures and I pushed Mavis around to the car. As I pulled up beside the car, I could sense both excitement and apprehension both with Mavis and myself. In some ways, we were like naughty schoolchildren and like them if you can get away with it, fine but if something goes wrong you are going to be in deep trouble. I knew we had not transferred to a car before but I thought we could manage that. The problem was going to be transferring from the car back to the wheelchair. The car was a lot lower than we had transferred from at any time before and the lifts had always been straight lifts i.e. with me in front. It then occurred to me that getting her out was going to be much more difficult than hopefully getting Mavis in was going to be, but we would cross that bridge when we came to it. I told Mavis what we were going to try and she agreed with me it was worth the risk, after all if it all went wrong Mavis would just land up on the floor and I would have to go and get help from the staff in the hospital. So I opened the car door, positioned the chair close to the car seat and go to the front of Mavis to make the lift. This does not work as the door is in my way to lift her, so I move the chair back a bit and change the angle. I whisper to Mavis that this is going to be it and lift. She stood on her right leg with her left leg in the air. This I had noticed before, and I was told by physio that for some reason the brain had shortened all the tendons in the left side of the body so the left leg was about 2" shorter. Still never mind we were both standing now, locked in this bear hug of an embrace and trying so hard not to collapse. I tried to shuffle around so that Mavis's bum would at least be pointing towards the car but then realised that the foot plates of the wheelchair were getting in the way; so I lowered Mavis down again into the wheelchair and we have a breather.

Yes! It still was a good idea, we just had to remove the obstacles. So, I took the footplates off the wheelchair. This does two things: it facilitates the 90o turn without getting Mavis's feet embroiled with them and also allows the wheelchair to be a little closer to the point of entry. We tried again and yes, it worked! Up, shuffle to the left, turn, and lower, and Mavis was now sitting on the car seat. I pushed her legs in and fastened the seat belt and we were off! Where would she like to go? Home! Therefore, to home we would go.

I reversed the car up the drive and decided that there was little point in attempting to get Mavis out of the car, as there was nowhere to take her. I couldn't get her into the house and in any case, we didn't have too much time, as Mavis might need the toilet and then what would I do? I popped in to tell Helen and help her outside and she sat in the back seat so she could talk to Mavis. The neighbours all came along to see Mavis holding audience from the front seat of the car and so we had afternoon tea/coffee on the drive, very much like any other garden party. After about half an hour, we said our goodbyes and started back to the hospital.

By the end of the road, Mavis was in tears and now I knew why they said you should not take people home. At least I thought it was but Mavis says it was tears of joy she is crying this time, because she made it home. This made me feel much better and I decided to concentrate more on how I am now going to get her out of the car when we returned to the hospital. We parked in the same area as before so that no one could see us if we made fools of ourselves. I lifted the wheelchair out of the boot and positioned it close to the door just to find that it does not give me enough room to reach down to get hold of Mavis in our famous bear hug. Back to the drawing board. We discussed it a little and then decided to move the wheelchair away from the car completely. This would allow us all the room we needed and so we tried again. I pulled her legs round so they are outside the car and Mavis put her arms around my neck and I put mine under her arms. One gigantic lift and low and behold she was standing. She balanced on one leg holding on to the car door while I moved the wheelchair into position and she then slumped down to complete the perfect transfer from car to wheelchair. We looked at each other in total triumphant relief and I pushed her back to the ward in time for a hasty rush to the toilet and then tea.

Sunday 29th August 2004.

It is a lovely day; Ailsa, Mark her husband and Henry the grandson have come to see Mavis. We sit outside the hospital, in the garden and I let slip to Mavis that our friends Polly and Ed had rung to ask us if we would like to join their church on a holiday to Norway. It would be the following July, so Mavis still has plenty of time to recover. The holiday was going to be by coach so I thought this would be a good idea. Mavis did not! After Ailsa and the family left, we discussed it thoroughly and I tried my best to persuade her. I lost the augment BUT it was great to lose it in some ways because during the discussion Mavis had been able to demonstrate logical thought sequence and reasoning. She might not have been able to express herself well because of her dysphasia, but her brain was able to present a valid, logical argument. This provided great hope for the future.

Tuesday 31st August 2004.

True to her word, the speech therapist brought in some simple crosswords for Mavis to do and some reading material in the form of children's books. Mavis was asked to read out loud and it did not make sense at all. The therapist and I looked at each other and then both looked over Mavis's shoulder as she reads. We both noticed that sometimes Mavis read the word incorrectly because the brain had interpreted it differently. More worrying was that when she moved her eyes from line to line, she always started in the middle of the row, seeing nothing to the left. This left sided deficit is quite often found in stroke victims, as although the eye can see it perfectly clearly; the brain for some reason cannot recognise it and shuts it out of the picture. Mavis was unaware of this and didn't know why the text did not make sense. Although worrying, it has been known to improve and therefore we comforted Mavis with this thought, telling her it is best if she concentrated on the crosswords instead. I left Mavis just before lunch telling her that I have to take Helen to the hospital this afternoon so I will not be back in to see her until tomorrow. She accepted this and I suggested she might like to try to do the crosswords in the evening before she goes to bed, as it will help to pass the time.

Wednesday 1st September 2004.

I arrived about 10.00 and Mavis is already in physio. I wandered down to watch the tremendous effort being put in by everyone to find out exactly what Mavis will be able to achieve. After physio, I wheeled Mavis back to her room and asked her if she managed to do any of the crosswords. She answered No, and when I asked why not she said that although she thought she knew the answers to a couple of the clues, they did not fit in the squares, so she must be wrong. I thought it might be helpful if we looked at them together so we started at clue number one. Now I know my general knowledge is very poor but after all, these are very simple crosswords, particularly we are told, designed for these very circumstances. Clue one 'What is the opposite colour to black' (5) I asked Mavis if she knew the answer "Yes White". Good I said and went to write it in the space but it would not go. Ok try another clue. 'A large white bird that has webbed feet (4)' "Swan" said Mavis. Good I said and tried to write that one in, apart from the fact there are six spaces to fill this time. I looked at several of the other clues and although Mavis knew the answers and I also thought they were correct, there was no way that these would fit the crossword. Fortunately, the speech therapist was in the building so I confronted her with some of the clues. She gave me exactly the same answers Mavis and I had thought of so it cannot be just us then. When I explained the situation to her, she admitted that she had just copied these out of a special speech therapist book and had not checked them herself. We huddled together trying to find the answers in the back of her book and yes, the answers to the clues were correct but the crossword had all the black squares put in completely the wrong places. She did apologise and went to explain to Mavis that it was not her fault. I visualised vast numbers of stoke survivors across the English speaking world now even more deluded because they couldn't complete a simple crossword. C'est-la-vie.

Thursday 2nd September 2004.

If Mavis was going to get out and about, even if she cannot walk again, it will be necessary to have some sort of mobility aid like an electric wheelchair or scooter. To pass the afternoon I suggested I load Mavis into the car again and we visit a mobility shop to see what they had to offer. What I had not bargained for was that on a Thursday, many staff are around changing shifts and this time we were spotted doing the transfer from the wheelchair to the car and reported to the head physio. Now, picking a mobility unit, whether wheelchair or scooter is no easy task. There had been loads of good advice on the web which I had spent weeks reading up on, but at the actual point of trying things, I was still worried about making the wrong decision. We went to the centre that one of the staff had told us looked after all the NHS stuff in the hospital, which seemed a good starting point.

We told them what we were looking for and they suggested we try a few. A good idea and after looking at them all, we decided to try two of them. The transfer was fine and Mavis steered the units round the shop with little difficulty. The problem was asking if we could take them outside or even take one home, to see if it would be suitable for the house. This idea was rejected outright and so we left. To anybody reading this who may be tempted to buy a wheelchair, do not do it until you have tried it under **all** situations. What works well in say a shopping mall, may not work at all trying to cross a busy road with a slightly steep kerb. Go to a company that will let you try the chair under all conditions. They realise that it has to be right for you and if the company will not let you do it, go somewhere else. There are plenty of companies that will.

Friday 3rd September 2004.

Mavis was taken down to the physio department and as usual, I followed her. What I was not expecting was to be called to the head physio's office and asked what it was we were doing yesterday. Although surprised at the question, there seemed little point in trying to disguise that we were doing a transfer, so I told her. She did not look too pleased but asked how we had managed. I told her it had all gone very satisfactorily but she insisted that, after Mavis had finished her exercises, we take her to the car and we could demonstrate. Nothing like being put on the spot then. I returned to the gym and when Mavis had finished told her what had happened. She looked alarmed but I assured her that if she tried hard I was sure we could manage it 'under clinical conditions,' and so the whole group of us walked round to the car. I whispered to Mavis that if she could manage it we could earn extra brownie points and see the look of determined will power enter her face. Preparations done, the wheelchair in the right position with the footrests off, our arms in a bear hug and 1, 2, 3 lift! Perfect, I shuffled round and pointed the bum in the right direction and lowered, then moved the legs into the car and shut the door. I now stood upright with a big large grin on my face saying, "I told you we could do it"! "Ok" said the physio "that's the easy part now let us see you get her out" I opened the door, gave Mavis that look that says it's all down to her now and unfolded her legs out of the car. Positioning the chair in the appropriate place, I entered the bear hug position. I must admit that I was expecting to have to summon up every bit of energy I could for the lift but to my surprise, it was a lot easier than it had been before and there we were both standing. We shuffled our feet round into the right position and Mavis slowly sank into the wheelchair. I reattach the footrests and look at the crowd. Chief Physio had a little smile on her face, the OT was beaming, and I think the ward nurse had tears in her eyes but that could have been the wind. We walked back to the ward and the chief physio asked me why we had not told her we had been transferring to the car. It was true that she hadn't asked us, but I responded by saying that if I had have asked her if we could do it, what would she have told us? "I would have said "No," she replied, "as I did not think Mavis would have been ready." Was it a good transfer I asked? "Perfect," she said, so we walked back to the ward.

Monday 6th September 2004.

Family meeting day! Now all the assessments have been completed, a council of representatives was held. These included Nursing staff, Doctor, Occupational Therapist, Speech Therapist and Physiotherapist, Heather, Ailsa, myself and of course Mavis. Each gave their report as to what they had found and what they expected to happen in the future. I think we all knew it was not going to be good but it really comes home to you when the head physio tells the meeting that Mavis will never be able to walk again and it would be very doubtful if she would ever be able to transfer on her own. The rest of the professionals concurred and Mavis cried. As such, the good news, if you could call it that, was that Mavis would automatically qualify for an electric wheelchair under the council's criteria; the bad news was that the waiting list was over a year! The meeting concluded and we went back to the ward. It was very hard to accept but if that was the experts' view then we had to accept it.

The next few days were filled with tension to say the least. We all had to come to terms with the hard facts that basically whatever movement Mavis had now was going to be the best she would have for the rest of her life. On top of the general disappointment, it also occurred to me that life was going to be very interesting when Mavis did come out of hospital as I would then have two people to look after, Helen and Mavis. Still, we would cross that bridge when we came to it, as Mavis's discharge still seemed some time away.

Thursday 9th September 2004.

After physio had finished in the afternoon, I decided that if we had to wait ages for an electric wheelchair to be provided by the NHS then Mavis and I ought to start looking for ourselves. We were lucky enough to have savings and so it was time to find out which chair would be the most suitable and how much it would cost. We had been recommended another company in Gateshead about ½ hour away from the hospital so off we went. They had a tremendous range in stock and we were able to try most of them. I had taken measurements from home and soon we could limit it down to three chairs, all of which they said they were prepared to bring to the house so that we could see if they worked in situ.

When we returned to the hospital, Mavis went to have her tea and I went home to attend to Helen. It occurred to me then that if Mavis was not going to be able to transfer on her own, then the sides of the wheelchair needed to be able to be removed in case you ever got into the situation where access to the front of the chair was extremely limited. Just another thing to think about.

Saturday 11th September 2004.

I think we were all feeling down this week, trying to come to terms with the results of the family meeting, so I thought it might cheer Mavis up if I took her home this afternoon. As this was against the rules, I made the excuse that I was taking Mavis out for a meal again and so we set off. I thought I had managed to get it all worked out. In the morning, our neighbour Bill and I had constructed five ramps that would get Mavis into the house. To do this meant going in through the garage and by using a ramp, we could go up the step at the back of the garage into the back garden. From the back garden, a small ramp would take us up a step to the back door. We had constructed a special ramp that would go over the threshold allowing us into the utility room, and from there we provided another ramp from the utility into the kitchen and another down from the kitchen to the main house. As we drove up to the house, I told Mavis what we were going to try to do, and so the escapade started.

First, I had to transfer Mavis from the car to the wheelchair. This we had done before so it would not be a problem. Well it was! All the transfers we had done before were on the flat and we were now finding out that trying to do a transfer on the slope of the drive was another matter. I put the car back down on the road and we started again! Simple..., not so. Alongside a road is usually a footpath, which is about 4" higher than the road and 4", is a lot when you are trying to lift a weight in excess of 16 stone from a car. Therefore, after three attempts and failing I decide to move the car away from the kerb so that Mavis could put her feet down on the road instead of the path. People would just have to think that I had a bad parking day. With the car now parked about 18" from the kerb and the wheelchair placed with its wheels precariously close to the edge of the pavement we did the transfer. Whew, what a performance! Still it would all be worth it once I had Mavis inside. Up with the garage door and in through the garage. I attempted a run at the first ramp to get us into the back garden. The little front wheels of the chair hit the wood of the ramp and instead of climbing onto the ramp and rolling up; it came to a dead stop nearly catapulting Mavis into the garden. OK, so we live and learn. Taking the chair backwards this time we arrived in the back garden and transverse the second ramp to the back door. Three other ramps negotiated in the same way and Mavis was sitting in the front room crying her eyes out.

There are sometimes when you think you can never win. The tears abated and I was told they were now tears of happiness to be inside the house again so perhaps I had won after all. Bill and Pat came along, together with Bob and Joyce from next door and we all entertained each other for a useful two hours. After they left Mavis was starting to look worried. Enquiring why, I was told that she needed to spend a penny, but she could not work out how she was going to get to the toilet. Thankfully, I had. When Helen came to live with us, we had an extension built over the garage that was a self-contained Granny flat with its own loo and shower. In addition, as Helen had started to deteriorate through age we had a stair lift installed two years ago. The plan was to wheel Mavis in her wheelchair to the stair lift, transfer her to the stair lift and once upstairs transfer her from the stair lift to Helens wheelchair and then from there to the toilet. It seemed simple enough but it had not been tried before. So, another journey began. Wheelchair transfer to stair lift was perfect; up the stairs in the chair lift to the top, but Helens wheelchair was now in front of the stair lift and we had never done an 180o turn before. I moved the wheelchair away and lifted Mavis off the stair lift, then with one arm supporting Mavis and Mavis holding onto the radiator at the top of the stairs for grim death (literally) I managed to secure Helens wheelchair with my foot and got it into the right place for Mavis to sit.

I was beginning now to consider why the hospital said not to take the patient home! Another lift and Mavis is standing next to the toilet ready to be transferred to it. The only problem is that I cannot hold Mavis upright and take her trousers and knickers down at the same time. Now what do we do? The task was answered as a gush of urine hit the floor. Mavis was crying and looking extremely upset. The actual time between Mavis first asking to use the toilet and when we arrived, had been over twenty minutes. Having been left with such a weak bladder, after being catheterised for so long, it was little wonder she had had the accident.

Never mind, we managed to sit Mavis down on the loo and with a lot of jiggling about managed to get her changed. We reversed the performance and returned Mavis back downstairs. A total time of one hour thirteen minutes, from start to finish. If life was going to be like this when Mavis came home permanently, then all our days were going to be spent on toileting exercise. It was beginning to become clear just how difficult the future was looking.

Next it was time for something to eat, so trying to make things as normal as possible, I thought we would order an Indian takeaway as we often did on a Saturday night. It sounded a great idea! We waited for it to arrive and it was duly consumed. Now I know the brain controls everything we do but I had never imagined how much. Within five minutes of Mavis finishing the curry, her bowels wanted to get rid of it and so we had a repeat of this afternoon's exercise with obviously much more serious consequences. Fortunately, (or unfortunately depending on how you view it) when you cannot do anything much for yourself your dignity suffers and Mavis had lost all her dignity in the hospital. We just reached the top of the stairs and Mavis could contain herself no more. She filled her knickers and this was the very first time I had actually allowed myself to feel sorry for her. She cried and I cried in a pool of diarrhoea and I think both of us were thinking what a bad idea it was for me to bring her home.

Never mind, on with the clean up, by which time it was after 21:30 and Mavis needed to be returned to hospital. From the toilet to Helens wheelchair, from the wheelchair to the stair lift, from the stair lift to the wheelchair, a quick goodbye to Helen who wanted to know why we had taken so long, and over five ramps back to the car. We transferred from the car back to the wheelchair and as I wearily pushed Mavis back onto the ward, all the staff welcomed her back and hoped she had had a super night out. If only they knew.

Sunday 12th September 2004.

Now that the house smelt nice again and all the carpets were clean, I decided to be a glutton for punishment and take both Mavis and Helen to church. I woke Helen up early, loaded her into the car with her wheelchair before going down to the hospital for Mavis and her wheelchair, and then took both to church. It was interesting to note that

Helen was not so pleased with the fact that she had competition, as she was not the only one in a wheelchair. After the service Mavis needed to use the loo, so the performance started again but at least the church had a proper disabled toilet. Up until now if Mavis had wanted to use the toilet in the hospital two members of staff had taken her and it was a simple transfer from the wheelchair to a special chair, which was then pushed over the toilet. We still had to work out the problem of how to use an ordinary toilet with only one person to facilitate. It was quite simple. I lifted Mavis from the wheelchair. She stood on her one good leg holding onto the grab rails on the wall. I then removed her clothing. She held onto me, and either was dragged or she hopped until she could sit on the toilet. This time our system worked well. I then reloaded Helen and Mavis back into the car and deposited them both back at their respective abodes, Mavis in time for lunch at the hospital and Helen to sample my cooking yet again.

Monday 13th September 2004.

It was still warm and sunny for the time of year. When I went to visit Mavis in the big ward she was no longer there; she had been moved into a room of her own. Thinking this was a nice gesture on the staffs' behalf I went to her room, which was a reasonable size, and I was then asked to go and see the ward sister. The reason they had moved Mavis into the side room had not been a benevolent gesture at all. After they had removed Mavis's catheter they had taken some tests and discovered that Mavis had MRSA. Fortunately, this was confined to the bladder. She had been placed on a course of tablets to remedy this; therefore, the room is basically for isolation purposes. We brought all her cards together to decorate the room the best we could. Mavis did not have a television in her room now so I made a note to bring in the small one from our spare room at home tomorrow.

Tuesday 14th September 2004.

I arrived at about 10:00 with the television. It was very hot in Mavis's room and I went to open a window only to find that none of them would open. On closer inspection, I found that they had all been screwed shut and some sort of notice was on the glass. The sun has so faded it that it could not be read, so I took myself to the nurses' station to ask what the reason was for not being able to open a window. It transpired that the wood in the window had rotted so much that the glass kept falling out and therefore, as a remedy, the glass had been secured in and the window screwed shut so that the frame did not fall apart and the glass come out again. Under normal circumstances, this would have been intolerable; but as Mavis's programme throughout the day was fairly busy with little time in the room except at night when it was a lot cooler, it seemed it was not worth making too much fuss.

What happened to all the multi million pounds Mr Blair said he had put into the NHS? Could someone please tell me? I think I found out where at least some of it went. Health and Safety! After asking about the windows, I had returned to the room and found the ward sister there talking to Mavis. Mavis was quite excited about having her own television but was now being told that she could not use it. On asking the obvious question why? we were told that because it was not a hospital appliance it needed to be checked over by the hospital's electrician. Once he had done that, he would place a sticker on it and it then qualified to be used in the hospital. Ok, so when was this going to happen? She could not tell me but she would ring the relevant department and they would put it on their list. Meanwhile Mavis did not have a television to watch. Oh the joys of red tape.

Every cloud has a silver lining or in Mavis's case, a golden one. As Mavis could not watch television in the evenings, it occurred to me that we could use the evenings to do exercises, provided the physios agreed and provided we could borrow the wooden standing frame. As Mavis had physio that afternoon it seemed a good idea to ask. They readily agreed and spent the session showing me exactly how to use it. At the end of the day, we took it down to Mavis's room. After returning to look after Helen I went back to load Mavis into the frame. I think the big difference between myself and the physios was that they had to protect themselves against Mavis suing them if things went wrong. I did not think Mavis could sue me so when the tears started and she said she had had enough I "persuaded" her to continue for a little bit longer and tonight was the start of a very long haul.

Saturday 18th September 2004.
This weekend, Polly and Ed and some others of the gang, John and Wendy, were coming to see Mavis so we needed to do something a bit

special. I checked with the Chinese restaurant close to the Italian we had gone to earlier and yes, we could get a wheelchair in there and so a table for six was booked. The gang arrived just about lunchtime and made a fuss of Helen, which was good as it was someone else apart from me for her to talk to. We all went down to the hospital then to see Mavis and had an enjoyable afternoon in the lounge. We brought Helen home about 5pm. I fed her then put her in her room for her to enjoy her evening and we went out again to pick up Mavis. Although the staff were becoming used to this by now, they still made it a very special occasion for Mavis. They made sure she was bathed, her hair was done, and a little make up from one of the nurses was applied so that when we all arrived she looked radiant. It was raining now though so we had to take the cars and it is surprising how wet you can become making a transfer! Still we had a beautiful banquet. It was past midnight when we crept Mavis back into the hospital. I think even the night shift nurses were woken up.

Sunday 19th September 2004.

What a lovely day. I collected Mavis from the hospital whilst John looked after Helen and managed to get her into his Land Rover and we all went to church. Afterwards Margaret and Keith were going to join us all for Sunday lunch and everyone mucked in preparing the vegetables and setting the table. I arranged for Mavis to use the loo just before we left church. Taking her to Helens loo was not going to be needed now until just before lunch while the vegetables were cooking giving us plenty of time. This visit we reduced the time down to a real 25 minutes so it is amazing what you can do with a little practice. Margaret and Keith arrived about 15:30 so we had a late Sunday lunch thoroughly enjoying each other's company. Be warned though before letting anyone else into your kitchen, make sure it is clean beforehand. I must admit I had not. Just keeping on top of things, I had forgotten to clean the inside of the oven. This oven was over 30 years old and had served us extremely well and like most ovens, no matter how well cleaned it had been over the years, it was now showing its age. To my everlasting shame, Polly and Wendy decided to start cleaning this oven after the Sunday roast and spent what seemed like the rest of the day on it.

Monday 20th September 2004.

The clan went home after breakfast and I changed the beds and put the washing out. I then went to the Post Office to ask for the form allowing us to claim for Mavis's disability living allowance. I took one look at it and decided to fill it in when I had more time. Mavis was so tired she could hardly keep her eyes open. I tried to find out why she was so tired; hadn't she slept well? It seems she had slept very well but she is finding that many people make her tired. I don't know why this should be, but made a note to ask the Doctor about it later this afternoon. He told us that this is often the case with stroke survivors especially when their brain is still repairing itself. He best explained it as if you were starting a new job. There is a lot to be leant and Mavis's brain was doing exactly that. It had to learn again probably using very different parts of the brain than those usually associated with their normal functions, and this was taking a heavy toll. The best way Mavis's brain could cope with this was to sleep.

Thinking about the weekend and how good it had been and how wet I had become loading Mavis into and out of the car on Saturday night, I turned my attention to the future and if we were out, particularly in the electric wheelchair how would we cope if it started to rain? I pondered the idea for a long time and came up with the solution that cycle capes might be the answer. A quick telephone call to Keith who owned a cycle shop and two were ordered and despatched.

I arrived home after the evening visit and instead of going for coffee to Bill and Pats as I usually did, I decided to sit down and fill in the form. I do not know who designs the questions or whether they are intentionally designed to try to catch people out, but the form is appalling and it takes ages to work through. Questions like "How far can you walk?" Answer '0'. Next question "How long does it take you to get there?" Therefore, what do you write in response? Where exactly is 'there' and if you cannot walk at all, then the time taken to get to 'there' seems pointless. I wondered if they were happy with the answer "infinity".

The rest of this week passed without incident at the hospital and probably for the first time some routine started to emerge. I had Helens social worker confirm that she had arranged for Helen to go to a day club on a Thursday and that the bus would pick her up about 09:00. This meant that she was out for two days per week now and she at least was fed properly those days. The other place she went to was the Cameo Club at Church. This was arranged through the local taxi firm who would come, collect her, and also take her wheelchair. The volunteers at Church would collect her from the taxi and look after her. They also arranged for a taxi to bring her home. This helped enormously as it meant that basically, it gave me two completely free days, not only to go to the hospital, but also to do the washing and clean the house properly. Helen was doing well with this although she needed a 'prompting' sometimes to go on a Thursday. She did not know the people well and I think some of the others smoked which was abhorrent to her.

Tuesday 21st September 2004.

I have decided that since Mavis is still without a television, I will again bend the rules a little. The morning was spent plugging in the aerial and retuning the television to pick up the signals from Sunderland, as we are on a different frequency at home. Mavis's exercises and assessments were still going on at the hospital. It was established that she did have a serious left side deficit and that although her mind was active, it did not always appear that way because of her quite bad dysphasia. This from a layperson point of view was quite interesting to behold. While Mavis was attempting to speak, you could see each word being selected from the brain before it would arrive at her mouth. I can only describe it like using the spelling checker in a word processing package. She would mostly be able to find a word, starting with the first one or two letters of the word, she wanted to use quickly. After that, it was just as if the brain would then try to open the dictionary to all the other words starting with these letters and would then methodically go through them one by one until it selected the correct one. It did mean that her speech was extremely slow. You had to be extremely patient, trying hard not to find the word for her or to finish the sentence. However, it often brought a great deal of laughter sometimes when the wrong words escaped.

Friday 24th September 2004.

I had a word with the OT helper in the hospital today as I was aware that there were many things that might be possible to help Mavis once she left hospital, if only you knew what and where to look. She showed me some leaflets that she had collected over the years. I could not understand why these were not offered to people, rather than being locked away, only to see the light of day when someone specifically asked. What I did find out was that there was such a thing as a RADAR key. This opens most if not all the disabled toilets in the country, but it did not tell you where you could get one, so something to look up when I returned home. The evening passed in the hospital talking with the other 'inmates' and their spouses and it was fair to say that we all felt we were in the same boat, with little or no information being forthcoming. In the room opposite us were Sharon and her partner Charlie. She was relatively young when she had a spinal stroke, while out with the girls one night, and it now looked as if she would never be able to move her legs again. Obviously, she was distraught and talking with them over several weeks it seemed they were battling over the same sorts of things we were. Charlie and I, along with another two husbands, were trying to find out what would happen if and when our respective partners were discharged from the hospital, and we agreed tonight that we were fighting an uphill battle as nobody seemed to know, or if they did, they were not about to tell us.

After leaving the hospital, I went along to Bill and Pats to have supper and to vent some of my frustration. About midnight I returned home and just before retiring remembered about the RADAR key and decided to look it up on the Internet. As it happened, our home page on the web is MSN and there right in the middle of the page was this very large headline "All you need to know about disabled persons grants and benefits". After a very short introduction, the main link took me to 'The Department of the Deputy Prime Ministers' web site and wow what a revelation! In all, there were 12 pages to be printed out and read very carefully.

Saturday 25th September 2004.

After last weekend, everyone was on a high. Helen was in good fettle, the weather was nice, and again I brought Mavis home. We knew that if we were going to travel at any time in the future then it looked as if we were going to have to change the car from a saloon to an estate. This way we could accommodate the electric wheelchair, the transfer wheelchair, the commode, and a suitcase in the car and still have room for Mavis as well as myself. We went to the garage as they were offering a special deal. They gave us all the facts and figures to mull over during the weekend. I had gone to the garage with a definitive specification, which was, "I want exactly the same specification car we had now except in an estate model." You would not have thought that would have been difficult would you especially as I had driven the specification in to show them! I think they saw me coming.

To take advantage of their special deal I had to buy a car that was new but already registered. The only one they could find in the country that had everything on it that mine had, also had a few extras that obviously I would have to pay for. With the spec of the estate and prices in hand, we left the showroom and went home to have something to eat. Only to make the same mistake again! Saturday night was curry night. It wasn't a hot curry or anything like that, normally the mildest that they did and before the stroke, Mavis had never had any reaction to the curries she had eaten. I will not bore you with all the messy details again but sufficient to say we never made it to the loo. This proved to me that it had to be the brain that was making this happen and therefore curries were off the menu forever in the future. Discussing it on the way back to the hospital we did recall that before Mavis had the children she just could not keep Liver down. She used to like it but it never liked her and used to make her sick. After having the children, all was fine and she regularly used to make liver and bacon before the stroke. We just could not remember how we had found out that she could eat it again, but concluded that somehow the brain had accepted the Liver whereas now it was rejecting the curry.

Sunday 28th September 2004.

I collected Mavis from hospital and took her home again. We spent all the afternoon pondering the new cars specification and the money they were going to charge for it. It had everything I had on the existing car but much that I do not, such as electric driver's seat with memory. Why would I need a memory on the seat, as there is now only me that can drive it? It also had the extra special audio equipment, now with seven speakers and even special amplifiers to hear the music in a special way. To somebody who grew up with rock and roll at about 200db my hearing at 59 is not perhaps as sharp as it should have been. Was it really worth spending money on these extras? We went through it again and it seemed to make sense but I could not make the figures add up properly. If they were true then I was getting a really good deal.

Monday 27th September 2004.

I went into the hospital again as usual but this time found the ward sister and asked her if she knew anything about the information that I had gleaned from the Internet. She gave me a few addresses and telephone numbers. I gathered from Mavis that the man from the hospital came to her room, saw that the television was working, said something on the words of "glad to see its working", and then left. Whilst it is not the end of the world to be without a television, it does help to wile away a few hours when in isolation in a hospital. I cannot help thinking that if I had not been prepared to plug it in Mavis would have not been able to see anything for over 2 weeks now.

We left the hospital in the afternoon and went to the garage to order the new car. As we went over all the figures again, I noted to them that I could not make their figures balance but, seeing it was such a good deal, we would go for it. It was after they had checked everything that one kind salesperson noticed the computer (well it is always the computers fault isn't it) had not added in the extras on the car so the price was now £2800 more than I originally thought. We had already committed our minds to the new car and logic told me I should have said no to the deal but in a moment of weakness although a little disgruntled I decided to still go ahead. (I will draw the reader's attention to this point further in the book.) Back to the hospital, and as the evening started, I wheeled Mavis into Sharon's room to ask Charlie if he knew anything about the various options available, producing the twelve pages I had printed out from the Internet and the information from the Nurse earlier in the day. No, he did not but he certainly wanted to find out.

Tuesday 28th September 2004.

The trouble with good news is that everyone wants to spread it around. Within seconds of me walking into the ward with the copy of the information for Charlie, two others who had been talking with Charlie earlier were now asking for a copy, or at least where to get it. Both their partners had also been hit by severe strokes and they were as desperate as me to know what could be done, and how. I promised to get it for them and went down to see Mavis. As I got to her room, she was just being wheeled out on the way to the toilet with two nurses, as it always had been. Just then, there was an emergency at the other end of the ward and they had to leave Mavis and attend urgently. It was up to me to take her to the toilet and I did not see why we could not manage it on our own. The experience we had had in church the Sunday before at last came into its own and we performed the whole operation easily. Transfer from the wheelchair at a point where Mavis could hold onto the grab rails near the bath. Mavis would stand there on one leg and I would lower her trouser bottoms and knickers. Still standing there in all her glory I would then get the commode chair and after getting it in the right position Mavis could lower herself and be wheeled over the toilet. Business accomplished it was then just a reversal of the procedure and Mavis was back in the wheelchair.

We were just leaving the room when the Nurse who was responsible for Mavis was passing down the corridor. She noticed that there was only me and commented that if Mavis could hang on for a few more minutes she would help me to take her to the loo. She was extremely surprised and a little curious when I informed her that the mission had already been accomplished. She asked for a demonstration. This we did and from now on only one person was needed! Mavis even remarked that this was even better as I at least took the trouble to make sure her knickers were comfortable after I had pulled them up. She then continued with a twinkle in her eye that most of the male nurses also did, it was only the female nurses that seemed to put them in such a position that they were uncomfortable.

In the evening Mavis and I had been in long discussions with Sharon and Charlie as to how we were going to a) progress and b) cope when it was time for discharge. I returned Mavis back to her room and started to prepare her for bed as I usually did before I went home to my empty one. Tonight as I took Mavis's shoe off she remarked that something on her foot hurt and could I have a look. For those of you with ticklish feet, God has a reason … Believe me. Mavis had always had very ticklish feet and as I was examining her left one, I must have caught a ticklish spot and Mavis moved her big toe. Now I must admit it was not a great movement, but I was sure it had moved so I asked her if she could do it again and, miracle that it was, it moved again. In fact, she could make it move three times more before it stopped. Mavis went to bed very tired but excited, and I went to break the cautious news to Bill and Pat.

Wednesday 29th September 2004.
I arrived quite early on the ward. Mavis had just had her bath and

was lying on the bed waiting for someone to dress her. I approached the bed with great trembling and anticipation and asked her about her foot. "No, it didn't hurt any more" she responded. "Not the hurt! Can you move your toes?" I almost shouted at her. I helped her sit up on the bed and she dangled her legs over the side. I was scrutinising her big toe when the Nurse walked in. "Is there a problem?" she asked "No," I replied "I am trying to see if Mavis can move her big toe again like she did last night" With that she got down on her knees and we were both looking with great scrutiny at Mavis's big toe. "Right" I said, "move it" and Yes it moved, "and again" I said and Yes it moved again. The Nurse got up and went to tell the sister who came and asked for a demonstration. Unfortunately, we only had one move left and it was only a little one at that, but we all agreed it was something to feel really pleased about and the nurse came with me to make sure that the physios knew all about it. They all asked to see it as well. Low and behold everyone was now interested in Mavis's big toe. It didn't move at all and try as she might nothing was going to make it move. The nurse, Mavis and myself were very despondent but the physios reassured us that we had probably just tired either the part of the brain that was asking it to move, the receptors that transferred the message from the brain to the big toe, or even just the big toe itself had just worn out. They suggested they try to look at it again tomorrow.

Thursday 30th September 2004.

Never before had I seen so many pair of eyes focusing on one big toe! Whether it was the power of concentration and everyone willing it to move I do not know, but it did. It resulted in something between a cheer, a gasp and a very big grin on Mavis and my faces. "Ok," said the physio, "now we have something to work with," and promptly put Mavis in the standing frame again. If the sensations are getting through then building up to twenty minutes standing was going to be essential.

Charlie popped in to the department as Sharon was having her physio at the same time and we decided that we both had to apply to the council to find out more about the grants that were available.

This afternoon we drove the old car to the garage to exchange it for the new one. It was supposed to have been ready for 16:00 but when we arrived there it still had its covers on and nobody seemed interested in attending to us. We waited and by 17:00 they came to tell us that they would not be long now as they had forgotten to tax it and they were just waiting for the person to come back with the tax. As soon as he arrived back, we dispensed with the formal handing over niceties and I rushed Mavis back to the hospital, as she was already late for dinner. It was only after I had rushed her back there that I had time to look in depth at the car I had taken. I was aghast to note that Yes, it had a lot of extras on that I didn't really want, but it also did not have a lot on it that I had on my other car even though they said it would. Yet another battle to fight.

Friday 1st October 2004.

I called at the garage on the way to the hospital to tell them of my dissatisfaction. They told me that as the car had left the showroom there was nothing they could do about it, which I found infuriating, as it was entirely their fault we had had to leave in such a hurry last night anyway. I arrived at the hospital and as I was in fighting spirit, I had a word with the hospitals OT about what if anything was likely to happen with the council. She said that we could expect to hear from them fairly soon and that she would have a word on our behalf because although a discharge date had not been set yet it wouldn't be very long, once they had decided where Mavis was going. This was indeed news to me. It had just never crossed my mind that when Mavis came out of the hospital she wouldn't be coming home. The OT told me that Mavis could not come home because from what we had told her, the house was not suitable. This meant that probably Mavis would be sent to a Nursing home. This was a huge shock and one I did not want to tell Mavis about yet but certainly, the efforts in the standing frame in her room every night took on a new urgency.

Saturday 2nd October 2004.

Technically the 3rd of October is Mavis's birthday but we thought that Saturday would be the best time to celebrate it, with a big family outside do and then a family Sunday lunch all together. Heather and all her family came up for the weekend and Ailsa and her family came across both for the evening and for all of Sunday. We took Helen down to the hospital, collected Mavis in her wheelchair, so now we have two wheelchairs to push along the ¾-mile or so, to the restaurant. The grandchildren loved it as we had races between the chairs and each had to have a turn at pushing either Helen or Mavis.

It was a lovely experience being all together and I kept thanking God that he had allowed it to happen, as it might have been so much worse. As it was, Ailsa's mother in law had been diagnosed with terminal cancer just a few weeks ago. For Henry to lose both Grandmothers in the space of such a short time, would have been horrendously traumatic for him. He was coping reasonably well but you could see it was taking its toll on the whole family not only Henry. Ailsa was coming over to see Mavis as often as she could usually two or three times a week and Mark was going to see his Mother as often as he could and poor Henry was going to both. We had a super meal and returned Mavis back to the hospital fairly early by our usual standards as the grandchildren were already well past their bedtime. The rest of us all returned home with Helen, and put her to bed as well, as she was exhausted from all the activity.

Sunday 3rd October 2004.

We picked Mavis up nice and early so that we could all go to church. She was showered with love and kisses from everyone and it made her feel very special. She told everyone at lunchtime how much she had enjoyed the time and that she was really looking forward to coming home. Was now a good time to tell her? Why spoil a good day. There was always going to be plenty of bad ones. I decided to wait until later in the week.

Monday 4th October 2004.

I went to visit Mavis this afternoon and the ward was a little glum. 'S' the lady who was devoid of any memory had left the ward and was being placed in a Nursing home down by the sea front. They had all said their goodbyes knowing that probably the nursing home was going to be S's abode for the rest of her life. Good news though the ward OT's had told Mavis they were going to start Mavis doing chores in the ward kitchen to prepare her for coming home and maybe also some work on the computer.

Wednesday 6th October 2004.

Mavis has to have a special test to make sure that blood is circulating around what is left of her brain properly, and so she had to go back to the Royal. I reached the hospital nice and early to see Mavis already in the chair with the ambulance men waiting to take her. She was loaded into the ambulance and as the doors closed, I noticed that tears were again streaming down her face. On enquiring why, I was told that it was because she does not want to go back to the Royal. It was an awful hospital and she hates it! I must admit it took some time to calm her down and it really brings home to me how much Mavis had been traumatised by her stay in there. Reluctantly she agreed it is for her own good to go. When we get there, she is a little bit more reconciled and the tests all go according to plan.

Thursday 7th October 2004.

It's raining today so it prompts my memory to take the cycle capes to show Mavis as they have been lying around the house now for a few days. As the ward looks dull and flat, after Mavis has had her physio, I put the capes on Mavis and myself and complete with Mavis in the Sou'wester hat we put on a fashion parade for the rest of the ward. Fortunately, nobody had any stitches in that would burst, as the sight of Mavis and I tripping up and down the ward lifted everyone's spirits a little, including ours. It was nice to see people laughing, instead of crying for a change.

Friday 8th October 2004.

I received a phone call from the council that a community OT would like to come out next week to see what can be done to the house to accommodate Mavis's homecoming. We arranged the visit for the following Tuesday and I looked forward in great anticipation. I explained this to Mavis but I still have not told her that there is still a very strong chance that she will not be coming home for at least another year.

Tuesday 12th October 2004.

10:30 exactly on time the doorbell chimed and a very petite young lady was standing on the step introducing herself as the community OT. She came in and we commenced our discussions of what she thought we needed and what I thought we needed. Unfortunately, it is soon very clear that we are poles apart. I had already done my homework. I had worked out how Mavis, either in her electric wheelchair or being pushed, could get in via the garage and once inside, providing we had ways of getting Mavis up or down the stairs to the bedroom/bathroom, then we could manage. Previously I had collected leaflets on through

floor lifts and had been to see one in the disability centre in Newcastle.
I had even contacted the company in Ireland that made the one with the
smallest footprint and checked all the sizes, to make sure it was viable.
I attempted to discuss this approach with her but it is fair to say that I
had never come across anyone so negative in their approach to someone's
rehabilitation ever before and I am afraid I told her so. If she was going
to be so negative, I did not want her in charge of Mavis's repatriation and
with that, I asked her to leave. She did.

Wednesday 13th October 2004.

I received a telephone call from the young lady's boss asking what
had happened yesterday, I expressed my total anger, and disapproval
at the sheer negativity of yesterday's meeting. The outcome was that I
could now expect a visit on Monday from a council surveyor who will
go through everything with me and we will try to find a way forward.
As I went into the ward this evening I passed the large notice board that
has all the patient's names and locations on it and I noticed something
slightly different about it. Next to Mavis's name is the announcement
'Discharge date 25/10/04.' My mind went into panic overdrive and it
asked so many questions I did not have the answers to, that my head hurt.
I hunted for anyone that could give me answers but as expected they had
all gone home, with only the night shift left and they could not tell me
anything. I asked Mavis if she knew anything but she did not even know
her discharge date was on the board.

Thursday 14th October 2004.

After Helen was collected for her day centre, I rushed to the hospital
to hunt out Sister. I found her in a meeting with the Matron from the
other hospital and we exchanged formalities. They gave me the courtesy
of plenty of time to ask many questions but the answers were not what
I wanted to hear. The good news was that the discharge date was 'only
provisional.' It was something to do with hospital and government
targets. It seems that under this set of circumstances the hospital sets
a 'realistic' discharge date. The other services then have to work to that
date and, if for some reason, Mavis cannot be discharged on that date;
her cost comes out of a different budget. I pointed out that nothing has
been done to sort out the house yet and they responded by giving the
bad news that Mavis would not be coming home but going to a Nursing

home once a vacancy became available. I argued this point very strongly and told them that if it is humanly possible I wanted Mavis to come home so that I could look after her myself.

From Husband to hospital visitor, to carer, to husband/carer.

One day I was a husband the next I was a hospital visitor. In the very early stages this was fine and I assume how it should be. The 'experts' were looking after Mavis and therefore you just went to the hospital each day when you could to see what was happening. Most of what was going on was outside of my control and I certainly was not privy to any decisions made concerning Mavis's recovery. It was only later, when things were not going the way I expected, that I started to intervene, but rightly or wrongly I felt it was still 100% the hospital's responsibility to get Mavis well again. Only after her move to Monkwearmouth, where I was actively encouraged to get involved, did it start to dawn on me that I was instrumental in determining her aftercare and recuperation. As I have tried to convey, by taking on the carer's role you have also to take on the responsibility that comes with it. With a disabled, vulnerable adult, this is enormous and extremely challenging, but only really hits you when you are both out of hospital and you have nobody else to help with the day to day matters. This is why it is so terribly important that carers get both the financial and emotional support they need. Sometimes the obstacles do become mountains and they just need some help coping with them. Worrying about financial difficulties is something they can do without. The first year was by far the worst because we were both struggling to find some sort of routine and I think without routine we can all feel vulnerable. Now we have fallen back into a life where each day is more or less the same, the burden of responsibility feels as if it has diminished to the point where I seldom think about it anymore. Dressing, bathing, cooking, cleaning etc has just become a way of life that we both accept, and we live like any other couple. As such the husband label is slowly replacing the carer label once again.

Chapter 8
Enter the Social Worker.

Friday 15th October 2004.

Now my impression of social workers was best summed up by a slogan once seen painted in a London tube station that read "Save a child! Shoot a social worker!" But somehow, 'V' was different. She was slim, elegant and knowledgeable and after my initial hostile feelings started to subside I started to warm to her. She listened carefully to what both Mavis and I had to say. She actually agreed with us that the best place for Mavis was at home, but in her opinion, the problems were huge and it probably could not be done. I asked her why not and she started to list all the problems one by one. a) How would we get Mavis into the house? I had to tell her then that I had built ramps and that Mavis had been coming now for the last 6 weeks. b) How would we get Mavis upstairs to bed? I told her that I would put in another stair lift and that by using her wheelchair and borrowing Helens overnight I could manage to get Mavis upstairs. c) What about personal hygiene? Well, a commode in the bedroom would solve most of that and I had worked out that if we put another commode in the cupboard under the stairs in the living room, Mavis could use that during the day. It was not ideal, but it was practical.

The only major point was could I give Mavis a bath? No, I could not; however I could give her a shower. By transferring her onto a bath board, she could sit on that with the shower curtain round her while I showered her. Again, this was not ideal, but certainly an awful lot better than she had received initially in the hospital. I was beginning to host the idea that 'V' was on our side. She was saying things like she could possibly arrange for Mavis to go to a Nursing home two or three times a week just to have a bath. Therefore, she left us with a promise that she would see what she would do. It seemed a very slim chance but one that both Mavis and I were determined to take. As she left the room, Mavis cried and cried. It had now been made very clear to her, probably for the first time, that her next move would not be coming home! Unless we could win the battle, it would be to a nursing/residential home until the house could be modified and the best estimation of that was that it would take at least a year. Not a happy time.

Saturday 16th October 2004.

I picked Mavis up from hospital and we drove over to the mobility company from whom we have decided to buy the wheelchair. This had been the company that had lent us various scooters, to try. In fairness to them, having given us such support, we felt it only right that they should have our business. Mavis tried another two or three and went for a spin around their factory unit. We decided on the one that could give lift as well as manoeuvre in very tight spaces and placed the order. It was bulky but it had to be in order to cope with Mavis and her weight. I took all the measurements and hoped it would fit into the new car.

Monday 18th October 2004.

'P, the surveyor from the council arrived. His attitude was refreshingly different from the community O.T. who visited last week. His ideas were positive and constructive. He actually seemed to know what he was talking about! We discussed at length what we thought would serve Mavis's need best. I walked him through my ideas, most of which he felt could work - but then he dropped a major bombshell concerning the through floor lift. Mavis was too young! If he had not before acknowledged that some of my ideas had carried some weight as being practical, I think I would have hit him there and then. Too Young! Mavis might look young but she was a pensioner. Didn't he realise that? He explained that the council for some reason would not sanction a through floor lift as they considered the useful life of a lift not much better than 10 to 15 years at best. This being so, it meant that if they spent the money now they might have to spend it again in another 10 to 15 years if Mavis lived that long, and they would not do that. Therefore I had a choice, either I let the council do it their way or if I insisted on a through floor lift I would have to pay for it myself. At £15k that was out of the question, we therefore looked at what plans 'P' could come up with. He went outside and measured the entire house, coming back about an hour later. We sat and looked at the drawing. 'P' thought the best way forward was to build a downstairs bedroom and wet room in front of the existing house. He was certain we had enough room but he would go away and consider it.

Tuesday 19th October 2004.

Helen's taxi came as usual to take her to her day club at church, and 'V' rang to say she wanted to come round to see the house for herself. She also said that she had been assigned as social worker to look after both Helen's and Mavis's needs. Mavis's electric wheelchair was delivered and I could, for the first time, make sure that it has enough room to wheel around all the corners, as it is much bigger than the transfer chair we have been using to date. If it was not for the fact that you had to be disabled to use one of these things, you could actually have some fun with them. I opened up all the doors, climbed in, switched on and away I went. Driving was simple and straightforward. On the tightest corner there was just enough room (on the second attempt) to move around. I hoped Mavis would find it as easy.

Mavis was doing well at physio now. Everyone was working very hard to try to enable Mavis to walk again but without much success. She was doing much better in her standing frame though. Both during the day and in the evenings she was now managing between fifteen to twenty minutes. We would inspect her foot every night to try to make the toes work. Sometimes they did, sometimes they did not, but the times they did not were becoming less so there was still hope! As Mavis's discharge date of the 25th was now imminent, I was trying to encourage the nursing staff to tell me what the chances were of Mavis being discharged next week. To be honest I do not think they knew or if they did, they were not telling me. I took a little comfort from the fact that all the others awaiting discharge were long over their discharge dates and therefore assumed it was unlikely to happen too quickly.

Wednesday 20th October 2004.

'V' came to see Helen and myself and we studied my plan of execution. It was perfect timing really, as now I could at least demonstrate the new wheelchair, showing how it would enable Mavis to transfer from the car on the road to the living room. I offered to give her a demonstration but she insisted on taking my word for it. I was starting to think that perhaps social workers were not as bad as I had once thought. It was of obvious concern to her that I would have problems looking after both Mavis and Helen, but to me it was straightforward. I had to cook for one so it made little difference cooking for three. Washing, cleaning was the same, the only problem I could foresee was that if something happened to one of them during the night, that necessitated a hospital visit, then the other was going to be left alone. She gave me an emergency telephone number that I could use if ever that did happen and said that as Helen lived in her own apartment of the house, she could arrange for someone to come and clean for her. This would just leave me the rest of the house to clean and would be of great help, as Helen was now having little 'accidents.' Cleaning her rooms, washing carpets etc., was becoming an almost daily task. So, we were nearly set. All I had to do now was to get a stair lift fitted and we could just pray that they would allow Mavis to come home.

Thursday 21st October 2004.

The man came to measure up for the stair lift. It was not too much of a problem until he mentioned the price. Our stairs are in three parts. From the hall, you go up three stairs to a small landing where you then turn right to go up the main flight. At the top, there is another small landing where you raise one further step onto the main landing, again at right angles to the stairs. To purchase a simple straight stair lift to go up the main flight of stairs was simple and about £1100, but to have a stair lift that went round the corner at the bottom with the three stairs and the one at the top was going to cost nearly £6000. This seemed an awful lot to pay when in about a year, hopefully, the extension to the house would be built and then we would not need it. I asked why so much difference. He told me it was something to do with the special track that is needed to take the chair around corners. It still seemed exorbitant to me.

We discussed a way of getting round the situation. I worked out that if I built a staging that effectively filled in the top landing then the stair lift could go right to the top. Providing there was room to place the wheel chair close to Mavis then I would be able to transfer her from the lift to the chair. This he agreed with, but it still left the problem at the bottom of the staircase with the three stairs. Now when I purchased the electric wheelchair, I knew it was going to be far too heavy to be able to lift into the estate car so, I purchased two ramps. Once Mavis was seated in the car, I could use the controls and drive the chair up these into the estate. Thinking that by using the two ramps inside now to drive the electric chair up the three steps to the landing to transfer Mavis to the lift seemed to be a good idea. Thus, the problem was solved. I ordered the simple straight stair lift and waited for its arrival in two weeks time.

Friday 22nd October 2004.

Before going to the hospital, I went to the garage for a meeting with the Sales Manager. Earlier last week I had written him a letter showing my dissatisfaction at being seriously misled. We had a long and very hostile meeting, to say the least. As 'compensation' he agreed to fit a proper mobile telephone in the car because they couldn't make my blue tooth adapter work due to all the special amplifiers for the all singing and dancing radio. He also agreed to 3 years free servicing for the car. Other than that, it was a 'take it or take it' situation and as there was little hope of any further progress, I decided to take it.

Saturday 23rd October 2004.

As my birthday was coming up on the 26th, Heather and her family drove up from Derby again to stay for the weekend and Ailsa and her family came across for the evening. We brought Mavis home in the afternoon. With great ceremony, Mavis was to try out her new wheelchair. Up the drive and into the garage, it worked well, and then up a ramp to manoeuvre from the garage into the back garden fine; up another ramp in the back garden brought her to the back door. After about six attempts with me giving instructions, she managed to drive through the back door and into the utility room. Up a further ramp and now, the really tight turn to get through into the kitchen. The footplates took away most of the plaster from the walls as we all tried to guide Mavis and the wheelchair. Eventually we did it and she was now incumbent in her own home, having achieved this more or less by herself, with a little help from her friends. After the grandchildren had become used to all the tears of joy shed by Mavis, they went to play on the stair lift and the rest of us had a good time catching up with everything that had happened. Of course, if Mavis could show off her new wheelchair; then I could show off my new car.

By this time, we were all hungry and in the interests of dignity, we were not going to have a curry. Instead, we had Pizza and chips. I had not realised before but most of the hospital meals did not include chips, not even when they had fish so, Mavis had not had many since her stroke, now four months ago. We bought a huge pack for us all to share and Mavis positively beamed with contentment. All her family around her and able to eat the food she liked. This was another simple example of the fact that we never really appreciate, the very simple things in life, until we cannot do them anymore. We took Mavis back to the hospital a very tired but very happy lady.

Sunday 24th October 2004.

Ailsa, Mark, and Henry went home last night as they all had commitments at their church today, so it just left Heather and her family. I went to the hospital to pick up Mavis while Heather helped Helen and we all met at church. Mavis could not say or do very much but she could worship and the strange thing was that she could sing and the words mostly were correct. This certainly was not the case when she was trying to talk. I can only assume that the words were coming from a different part of the brain, when she was singing, as she already knew most of the words whereas, when she was talking, or trying to, it needed different processes that had been damaged. We all came back home for Sunday lunch and the family left shortly afterwards to go home. The weekend had involved a great deal of very hard work but it had been absolutely wonderful with everyone able to be here for at least some of the time. In the evening when we returned, I think Mavis was asleep even before we got her into the hospital let along into bed.

Monday 25th October 2004.

There is still no news of what is going to happen to Mavis on discharge, or even if they have decided to let her come home or not, so life just has to go on in its present vein. Ailsa arrived early at the hospital as she was going to take Mavis to the Metro centre today, with Henry, to buy Mavis a special outfit for her cousin's youngest sons wedding. It was going to be held in Chalfont St Giles on November 6th but we did not think we would be able to get there. However, we checked it all out with the consultant and nursing staff. They all seemed to think that if I thought we could manage then we probably could. Ailsa took Mavis off and I went home to catch up on some work and spend a little time with Helen.

When I reached home, I went upstairs to see her and she looked in a fairly agitated state. It did not take long to ascertain that for some reason the toilet had overflowed. The toilet had never overflowed before. All the rest of house sewage systems were in working order so I concluded it must have been something she had either put or dropped down the bowl. I mentioned earlier that the last mini stroke had distorted her logic and reasoning powers and this was to be another fine example. In order to clean up the mess and the water it had occurred to her that the most suitable thing to use was the vacuum cleaner. Now I know you can get both wet and dry vacuum cleaners but I am afraid ours was not one of them and I gathered it had just gone bang as I had driven up the drive.

When I returned to the hospital Ailsa, Henry and Mavis were there showing all who would look, Mavis's new clothes for the wedding.

Tuesday 26th October 2004.

Gosh, I feel old today! Still life goes on and I show Helen off to her club before opening the post. A little bit of a shock here. We have a letter from the council. They are saying that as they have been informed Mavis will be coming home and, as I can manage to lift her upstairs, they will not be going ahead with the building development, as she would not qualify. This is very serious because although I think we can manage for a short time, to continue long term is going to be a nightmare. I contacted 'V' our friendly social worker again and she came round to see me. We discussed in full exactly what I had planned for Mavis. She agreed with me that it was Ok on a temporary basis but as a permanent way of life, it was a non-starter. 'V' looked at all the possibilities and then said she would contact the council on my behalf. I returned to the hospital where I was told off by Mavis for arriving late. She had bought a birthday present for me yesterday while at the Metro Centre, and it seems she had been longing to give it to me. You cannot win them all.

Wednesday 27th October 2004.

I get a call from 'P' the surveyor who tells me they have been speaking to 'V' and that it will be Ok after all. If Mavis does come home and I can prove it is only on a temporary basis then the building work will still be able to go ahead. I think he was a little shocked when I asked for conformation in writing.

Thursday 28th October 2004.

This morning I spoke with the sister on the ward and I asked if they are any nearer finalising Mavis's release. She told me they were still negotiating with the social workers but if everyone agreed, it could be next week. The day is cold outside and I think that over the last weeks we have visited every venue that it is possible to visit within pushing distance of a wheelchair. Boy, am I fit! So this afternoon I suggest to Mavis that we could play Scrabble and I am pleased to say she agreed. She used to get scores in the 200's, so I was interested to see what she could accomplish now. 74 against my 143 was not bad at all. It was becoming even more apparent that just because Mavis could not speak the words, her brain could find them in there somehow. It just took much more time for them to come out. Still, thinking time for her was thinking time for me also, so at least we were both happy improving our game.

This week Ailsa's Mother in law died and I really felt for George her husband who had nursed Beryl over the last months, virtually on a full time basis. This made me think how close I had been to burying Mavis a few months ago but now, instead, it was George.

Friday 29th October 2004.

Today was warmer so we decided we needed to go to town to do some shopping. The OT has suggested that Mavis might like to try a sport bra, as she should be able to put that on one handed. Now without being disrespectful to anyone, the OT has a bust that is lucky if it is half a handful, Mavis on the other hand, has always been well endowed. Whether these 'one fit all' bras will work for Mavis is doubtful but we have to try. I pushed the chair up to the town centre and we toured around all the various department stores asking if they had a bra that can be put on only using one hand. Needless to say, there was not a great abundance of them. In fact, we only managed to find two, and they did not look as if they would hold a picture up, let alone anything else. We sat in the mall eating an ice cream and just watched the world go by. When you take time to see what is actually going on it is surprising how many wheelchair bound people there actually are. It is also very surprising to see how inconsiderate others are towards them and their carers. I suppose we have this to come.

Saturday 30th October 2004.

I brought Mavis home again, but this time via the Metro centre. We had received a circular through the post showing some very nice chairs that I think will be ideal for Mavis when she does comes home. Our existing three-piece suite is quite low and so old it could do with being replaced. What better time to force the issue. We arrived at the shop and looked at the chairs. They were very nice and I transferred Mavis from her wheelchair to the chair. They appeared to be extremely comfortable but we decided that they were still too low and if I am going to have to do the transfers, we need a chair that is going to be as high as possible. It is very strange within a large furniture shop, watching all the other customers watching you to see what was going on as we transferred from one chair to another to another, using the wheelchair in between. Eventually we noticed a leather suite that was very high. Having tried it, we decided this is going to be the best that we can find (or afford). After making all the arrangements and visiting the shops disabled loo, we headed home, as it was nearly dinnertime.

This evening we had a Chinese meal instead of an Indian and again everything worked well. It was raining as Mavis and I negotiated all the ramps to get her back out of the house and into the car. We were both rather wet by the time we set off. It was another new experience for us as so far I suppose, we have only ventured out of the hospital if the weather has been fine. When it is raining, it does seem to take a long time to move from the chair to the car and then stow the chair in the back. Still again, I suppose it is something we will eventually become used to.

Monday 1ˢᵗ November 2004.

I set off early for Beryl's funeral as it was being conducted in Workington, about 3 hours drive away. I arrived at the church with about twenty minutes to spare and tried to find somewhere to park the car. There wasn't any parking for what seemed miles but when I asked someone, they said that if it was a funeral, then the wardens usually turned a blind eye for about 45 minutes. I left the car with a notice on it and hoped for the best. When we emerged from the church some seventy-five minutes later, I was relieved to observe that I did not have a ticket and followed the hearse to the cemetery. It had been a cold and wet journey to this side of the country but as we came out of the church, the rain had stopped and the sun was trying to break from behind the clouds. By the time we got to the graveside, the sun was shining and the air was full of autumn sweetness. The light played on the different coloured leaves and the sea had lost its cold clamour. I could see the lost look in George's eyes and felt how lucky I was that God had spared Mavis even for a little while. Ailsa and I swapped glances and probably thoughts as well, both knowing how close Mavis had been to death and both fighting this huge emotional turmoil that Mavis had lived whereas Beryl had died. I was wondering whether George and Mark were both feeling the same, but perhaps cheated and looking from the other end of the telescope.

A new week and there was an air of excitement building in the ward, as everyone knew that Mavis was going to go to a wedding at the weekend. This was balanced by my apprehension on exactly how we were going to manage and I did not dare ask Mavis. Friday arrived and I was in bright and early to collect her. We were both given strict instructions from the staff about Mavis's medication and what we should or shouldn't do.

Just before 11 o clock on *Friday 5th November,* we embarked on another unknown adventure. I must admit to great fear on Mavis's behalf and trepidation on mine. I assumed that it was because Mavis had been catheterised for so long that she now had an extremely weak bladder. When she said she wanted to go, this meant now, not when I felt the time would be more appropriate. The next time you are waiting outside a disabled toilet and you hear the hand dryer going on and on for ages, I can assure you that it is probably not that people keep drying their hands but it is that they are probably drying their knickers. Not particularly eco friendly as it takes a lot of electricity to dry one pair of knickers, but you can tell from the smile you get as you put on one pair of warm dry knickers rather than the cold wet ones you removed nearly half an hour ago, the added cost to the environment is well worth it.

We travelled down for the rest of the day from Motorway service to Motorway service and eventually reached the hotel about 17:30. I unloaded and reassembled the wheelchair and Mavis drove to reception. We had booked a disabled room and in fairness to the hotel they had given us, what they thought was a disabled room. It was wide enough to manoeuvre the wheelchair in the room and around the bed, but as with most hotels, it still had a bath with a shower above it so Mavis getting a bath or a shower looked as if it was going to be out of the question. I unpacked and Mavis had a rest on the bed. At about 20:00 we went down to have an evening meal also to discover who else from the family was staying. It seemed almost everyone, so the dining room was loud with merriment and I was so thankful that Mavis had been well enough to come. It might be extremely hard work for me, and very tiring for her, but it was the start of her re introduction into the world outside of hospital, albeit a very different one. During our meal Ailsa, Mark and Henry arrived so they joined us at our table and it was agreed that after breakfast the next morning, Ailsa would come down and do Mavis's hair and apply her makeup. Why is it that daughters seldom trust their fathers to accomplish such things?

Saturday 6th November 2004.

The night has gone reasonably well with me only being woken up three times to take Mavis to the toilet but we had managed well. After breakfast, as planned, Ailsa came and did Mavis's hair and makeup. We then dressed her in her finery. Now I know it was a wedding and the bride was supposed to be the centre of attention and the most beautiful woman there, but once Ailsa and I had finished with Mavis (well Ok Ailsa really) Mavis looked fantastic. So we ventured out into the world of the disabled and began to understand exactly how difficult it was, particularly how dreadful it must be, if you are disabled and on your own.

When we arrived at the church, we were told that the 'disabled' entrance was at the back, as it was easier to get a wheelchair in through the wide door at the rear. The only thing was, nobody had noticed that to reach the door at the rear, there were several steps at the side of the church that had to be negotiated. I returned to the car and unpacked the ramps, we then began the time consuming torture of going up one stair, moving the ramps, going up another stair, and so on until we arrived at the back of the church that was really at the side but very close to the altar. Due to this delay, we were running a little tight for time. The organ started playing the arrival music and I think many people were surprised when the side door opened and in came Mavis with her entourage instead of the bride, but they quickly realigned their gaze and the wedding ceremony went ahead without any problem.

We went back to the hotel for the reception and a fabulous time it was too. The only hurdle was that to reach the function room where the reception was being held, the staff insisted that it would be better for Mavis and the wheelchair if she went outside and around the grounds, then in up a small ramp they had put down to access the room. Like me, I do not think they had realised that this meant negotiating the wheelchair over some quite damp grass and up a reasonably steep slope (for a wheelchair anyway). If there is a sport for off road electric wheel chairing, then Mavis needs to enter. She tried it the sedate way and managed to reach about halfway up before the wheels started to spin. At my suggestion, she took it back down again and took a much longer run at it. With the chair doing all of its 4 miles an hour, it attacked the grass bank with great aplomb. Grass and mud were flying everywhere, including assaulting a few of the less aware guests standing nearby, but Mavis reached the top and proceeded into the function room. It was a shame about the nice grass bank that now had 2" tyre tracks at various degrees all over it, but thankfully, it was November. With a bit of luck next year's growth would disguise the grooves.

After the dinner, Mavis was tired and we retired to the room for what I thought would be for the rest of the night but, after about a two-hour rest, Mavis was keen to attend the rest of the evening and so we tried out "discoing" in her wheelchair. What a great little mover.

Sunday 7th November 2004.

Mavis must have been very tired as she slept all the night through until 07:30 when it was time to get up anyway. The hotel had been very good in supplying various 'aids' in the room to help in any way they could. One of these was a bathing stool, so it looked like a good idea for Mavis to have a bath. We worked out that if I lifted Mavis she could transfer from the wheelchair to the side of the bath. I would then stand in the bath and lift her from the side onto the bath stool in the bath and we could then fill the bath. In my defence this worked extremely well, it was just that I had not given much thought as to how I was going to lift her out, thinking it would be just a reverse procedure.

Well it wasn't. To begin with the bath was now extremely slippery and therefore Mavis lost all confidence in me being able to support her. Skin also seems to become very slippery after a bath even when it is almost dry. We tried various ways but none of them seemed to be working and I had this thought that Mavis's dignity was again going to suffer if I had to ask Mark, and perhaps a few porters, to give me a hand. There had to be a way. We stopped struggling and decided to sit down and reappraise the situation. This time I took the towels, completely dried Mavis, and then, using different towels, dried the bottom of the bath. I then went into the bedroom and borrowed the mat from the side of the bed. Putting that in the bath made a steady surface for Mavis to stand on as the mat could not move, and after one almighty heave Mavis was now standing on her one leg. I then used the pillows from the bed to line the top of the bath and lowered Mavis onto the pillows. This made the swivel of her feet from inside to the outside of the bath relatively straight forward and behold after one and a half hours, Mavis had had a bath and was now back in her wheelchair. This is exactly the way to build up an appetite for breakfast.

We went down to breakfast and most of the wedding party were there already, but it was a great time and we were both really pleased we had managed to go. Afterwards, I packed up the cases and the wheelchair, waved goodbye, and started for home. It was fairly early when we approached the M18, so I decided to give Margaret and Keith at Bridlington a ring and see if we could do a slight diversion and call to see them. Yes, they were in so about 16:00 we arrived in great fettle. I knew they had a downstairs toilet, so I had not expected any problems, but again, until you have to be made aware of problems, you seldom are. There was in fact one step from the hall down to the kitchen and then to the toilet beyond. There was also a step at the front door to get into the house. With Keith's help, we managed both well and Mavis and I had a very enjoyable tea with our hosts.

As we left, it occurred to both of us I think that as things stood, Mavis and I would never be able to go and stay with them for weekends as we had often done in the past, as there was no way we could manage the stairs at bedtime. Another one of those things we would have to get used to. As I was driving over the North Yorkshire moors on the way back, things were beginning to make a big impression on me, probably for the first time, as to what a huge responsibility I was undertaking. I had not broken down for years in a car but the little demons start to work in your brain. What if the car broke down now? How would I cope? Could I cope? As the streetlights of Teesside shone on the horizon, I settled down a bit and by 22:30, we were pulling up at the hospital. As I wheeled Mavis in, all the lights were out as everyone was at least in bed, if not asleep, and only the two night staff were visible. We put Mavis into bed and I went home very tired but rejoicing in the fact that the weekend had been a wonderful experience.

For the first time, we had been able to judge how we would manage in the real world and apart from the bath experience; all had gone reasonably well to plan. We had learnt that even when people say that access is easy, to always go and look for yourself, as one small step can hinder even the best of intentions.

I called in at Bill and Pats who were very eager to know how the weekend had gone. I also checked on how Helen had coped, as they were keeping an eye on her for me. It seems that they had invited her along to their home for a meal on the Saturday evening. She had stayed in on the Sunday with Pat feeding her again for lunch. We could not have gone away and left Helen without their help so again we were eternally in their debt.

Monday 8th November 2004.

I went up and checked with Helen before going to the hospital and she regaled me with everything that had happened over the weekend. She had really enjoyed her time with Bill and Pat and seemed full of life and confidence. She was much more like her old self. On arrival at the hospital, everyone was saying how pleased they all were that Mavis and I had had such a great weekend, so Mavis had obviously been telling everyone. I was suddenly brought back to reality when the ward sister came to see me. After discussing with her our experiences over the weekend and saying all had gone well, she said that Mavis was going to be discharged next Monday. I quizzed her about where Mavis might be going and she said that from what she could see, Mavis would possibly be allowed to come home. Now I knew that sometime Mavis would be discharged, and I was really pleased that she was now going to come home, however it still came as a shock and again the huge responsibility hit me. At least when you are having a baby you have nine months to adjust and even then, they are so small you can carry them around. Mavis was going to be a very different kettle of fish and now my idealistic way of us surviving was going to be put to the test in many ways.

Tuesday 9th November 2004.

Mavis's discharge had permeated through all the departments involved in her care. This week was more tuned into exactly what Mavis could or could not do so that her final assessment could be made. Physios were taking me through all the lifting positions and trying to make sure I did not damage myself by doing something incorrectly. 'S' from occupational therapy came to see me and arranged to come to the house on Thursday for a complete assessment for hand rails, grab rails, bath boards etc. Suddenly I was being overtaken by the system affording Mavis's discharge. The more they told me of the things I was going to have to do, the more it seemed I had forgotten. Trying not to panic I let them have their say and all seemed to progress nicely ready for the 15th.

Wednesday 10th November 2004.

I went up to see Helen as usual. She was still a little bit dopey this morning so I left her sleeping and went to the hospital. Returning home, I noticed she was not down stairs yet so I went up to see why. She was just waking up which was most unlike her and said she felt a little bit dizzy so I helped her get dressed and brought her down to give her lunch. She demolished her food well enough so I assumed she was Ok and returned to the hospital. Mavis and I played scrabble again and this time Mavis won. Not by a lot but she still won so things still seem to be improving in her brain. Later, she was taken along to the kitchen again so that they could reassess if she could make a cup of tea/coffee on her own without endangering herself. After that she was taken back to physio. All the long evening sessions of Mavis practicing in the standing frame were now beginning to pay off. She was now able to stand, albeit for a very short time on both legs, and with a great deal of assistance, could now take two steps. It was not quite Neil Armstrong's "one step for mankind" scenario but it was still very significant.

I went home to tell Helen who did not really seem to be interested. I fed her and she said she would rather go to bed straight away rather than later, as her legs did not feel right. After checking she was in bed Ok, I went back to the hospital for the evening session. I started talking to 'D' whose wife had had a stroke during an operation and she could hardly move at all. I knew he had been fighting various people for help in getting his wife home and today it all came pouring out. It seems that the care package was now place. They were just awaiting confirmation that the helpers, who would go into his house in the morning to help his wife be hoisted from the bed into the bath and then into a chair, were available. The hoist had already been ordered and was about to be installed and he was demented. He was telling me that the help was going to come in the morning and then at night to put his wife back into bed and obviously, he had asked various questions. One of which was "can you show me how the hoist works so that I can move my wife during the day should she need to go to the toilet?" It seems he had been told, in no uncertain terms, that he must not touch the hoist under any circumstances. If she needed to go to the toilet then she just had to do it where she was and she would be cleaned and changed when the staff came to put her to bed at night. This being totally unacceptable, he had complained, and was told that if there was any evidence that he had been using the hoist himself, it would be taken out of the house completely. He had been so shocked by this that he had not asked the next obvious question like "So if you take the hoist out completely how will the others be able to transfer her both morning and night?"

Charlie, Sharon's partner, then came down the ward and seeing what was going on also stopped so that 'D' could explode all his anxiety onto us. The poor guy was in a terrible state and nobody had ever seen him like this before. I suggested he make urgent contact with both the Matron and his social worker to see if a resolution could be worked out. It did seem completely unreasonable to expect his wife to have to sit in a soiled 'nappy' for anything up to 10 hours.

I left Mavis and on getting home went upstairs to check on Helen. She was sitting on the floor at the side of her bed and on enquiring why she was there, she told me she had just slipped out of bed and could not stand up again. I lifted her up and helped her to the toilet before putting her back to bed. I then went to bed expecting to sleep all the way through as usual. All the years Helen has lived with us we have always had a system that, if she needed someone in the night, she could press the intercom system on the telephone at the side of her bed and it would awake us. Never having been used before I was very surprised when I was awoken from my slumbers at about 01:30 by the telephone ringing. I answered it but heard nothing so I was a little bemused as to what was going on when I remembered it might possibly be Helen. I made myself decent and went up to her room to discover that again, she was sitting on the floor and supposedly, the same thing had happened. She had got up to go to the toilet, again her legs had given way leaving her slumped on the floor. After putting her on the toilet and then back to bed, I retired myself hoping to catch up on the lost sleep, but again about 04:15 the same thing happened. She seemed Ok in herself, but in her words, she kept feeling dizzy and would either fall or slide off her bed onto the floor. I put her back to bed again and not hearing anything else overnight, I went up to see her in the morning.

Thursday 11th November 2004.

I found Helen in the corner of the bedroom asleep, covered with the quilt that she had managed to pull from the bed. Assuming it best to leave her there, I telephoned for the doctor and he soon arrived. He checked her all over and said that as far as he could see there was nothing wrong with her. However, he was a little concerned that when we lifted her back into bed she complained that her hip hurt. Only to be on the safe side he was going to call for an ambulance and have her taken to hospital to have the hip X-rayed to satisfy himself that she had not damaged it. The ambulance duly arrived and carried her out to take her to hospital and I followed in the car. Never having done this all my life until five months ago, this was becoming an unfortunate habit.

It was only the suspicion that perhaps Helen had hurt her hip that probably saved her. Within hours of being admitted, she was fighting for her life with a very high temperature and complete delirium. It seems she had contracted pneumonia somehow and by two in the afternoon, she was indeed in a very serious condition. The doctors were all very concerned. In the hope that it might arrest the situation, they were pumping Helen with as many antibiotics as she could manage. Helen had no idea what was happening and so I left her and went to see Mavis in the other hospital. I now had this dilemma, did I tell Mavis or not. She did ask me why I was late so I thought a compromise was in order. Yes, Helen was in hospital and she was on a ward for observation after possibly damaging her hip. It told enough for Mavis to be concerned but not too much that she would panic and feel that somehow she had to go and see her Mum. I rang both Heather and Ailsa to keep them informed and Ailsa said she would come over on Sunday. I really felt sorry for her as over the last 5 months she has seemed to do nothing other than go backwards and forwards between Carlisle and the hospitals. Just as it looked as if everything was beginning to subside again into normality, it all flares up again.

Friday 12th November 2004

The house is empty again and as I arrived at the hospital to see Helen, it occurred to me that perhaps God has had a hand in this. It seemed a cruel thought but maybe God knew that coping with both Helen and Mavis when she comes home next week would be beyond my capabilities, even though I was willing to try. My thoughts went along the lines that possibly he had removed Helen to a place where she would be better looked after in both the short and longer-term future. I did worry that Helen had effectively been in my care, and what had I done to allow her to catch pneumonia. The doctors tried to reassure me that these things do happen sometimes without any obvious cause so I must just take their word for it.

Saturday 13th November 2004.

I collected Mavis from the hospital as usual to take her home for some lunch after which we went to the other hospital to see Helen. I had to tell Mavis now what she was expected to see and sure enough when we reach the ward, Helen had a mask on and was hooked up to all sorts of instrumentation. The Doctors told us that although it was very early days, Helen's temperature has stabilised and that there was a chance she might survive. We came home and with spirits being low, I invited Bill and Pat around for supper. This is good because the focus of conversation turns to Mavis's homecoming rather than dwelling on Helens situation. It also highlighted the fact that our bed was always on the low side and that to make it easier for Mavis to get in and possibly out it would be better if it was raised a little. We left Mavis with Pat while Bill and I went to his house where he had accumulated some 40 bricks from doing some work in his garden during the summer. A quick wheelbarrow full, plus a few grunts and groans, and our bed was now raised some 16" and looked like one of those Edwardian beds where you need a stepladder to get in. We finished supper and I returned Mavis to the hospital at about 23:15. We crept in and as silently as possible, I helped prepare Mavis ready for bed. As we kissed goodnight I thought I only have to do this for one more night and then she can be in our own bed and I will have someone to cuddle to keep me warm again.

Sunday 14th November 2004.

After church, Ailsa and Henry arrived. We all went to the hospital to see Helen. Henry is very upset this time, far more than usual and bursts into tears. I think losing his Gran and now it looking as if he might lose his great Gran, is proving all too much for the little fellow. We tried to reassure him that Helen is slowly getting better and that she is not going to die, well not yet anyway! Ailsa and Henry went home after having something to eat at our house. I then took Mavis back to the hospital. All the night shift staff made a huge fuss of saying goodbye to her and intimating they hope not to see her again. Lovely though they have been, I am sure the feeling was reciprocated. I went home to whizz round with the duster and vacuum cleaner. Not that the house was dirty, it wasn't, but it just seemed a ritual gesture worth going through. It might enhance her homecoming if Mavis did not see dust or bits on the carpet. Daft I know but there we go... sometimes we are.

The Child Parent relationship.

As we age there comes a time when we need to be looked after. There is never a defined time when this happens but slowly over the years, the ones you used to care for so indulgently slowly start to reciprocate the process, we hope with the same amount of indulgence. That is unless the circumstances change radically fast as they did in our case. Both daughters had left home and had families of their own to tend, but suddenly there was a situation at their parents' home that deeply affected them. Heather in Derby had the distance to contend with. With a young family, it was just not feasible to attend the parental home easily and therefore visits had to be planned well in advance. Ailsa on the other hand could more easily slip in a visit if time in her busy schedule allowed. So while Heather had to come to terms with the guilt of not being able to help very much on a day to day basis, Ailsa had to try to juggle her time between her own life, family and ours. In the early days, this was difficult for all parties. Heather helped by ordering and sending aids that would help Mavis such as a fork/knife (a bit like a pastry fork but with a sharper edge so that you can cut proper food, not just pastry). Ailsa came to help me with the VAT, income tax returns, etc as well as visiting her mother. I can clearly see that in the back of both their minds would be the question "what if this happens again." Certainly, at one time I did feel a little under pressure with jibes like," if you lived a little closer to us then....." and the odd suitable property that was for sale within their areas was sent via the internet. However, this has subsided and I have managed to reclaim my own decision making lifestyle. Yes, it would be very nice living closer to them, but thankfully, we can both be independent again as a couple and long may it remain so.

Chapter 9

Mavis is released.

Monday 15th November 2004.

I rang the hospital to see how Helen had been and I was told she has had a comfortable night so I have no need to worry about her. I went to Mavis's hospital and took with me a small case for all her belongings she had accumulated over the last five months. I took the cards off the wall and suddenly the room that had been her 'home' looked very stark as if it was giving up a long time friend. I carried the television back to the car by which time Mavis has been toileted and was ready to go home. In the office sister went through all Mavis's medication and gave me a copy of her care plan. We said our goodbyes to everyone and I started to push Mavis out of the ward for the last time. As we got to the end of the corridor, I took a deep breath and realised that from now on, I was on my own, and Mavis was totally in my care. I have used the analogy of bringing a baby home before and yes, like it or not, Mavis was going to be my big baby!

I drove the car to the drive and went to fetch the wheelchair. We did the transfer from the car to the wheelchair and Mavis drove it in. I noticed, as on previous occasions, that she had some difficulty driving in through the door, always hitting the left side, and by now, most of the plaster on the wall of the very tight corner had gone with only the bare bricks remaining. At one time that would have bothered me, but somehow I found that all my life's perspective had changed and those little things have become very insignificant. Mavis was home and that was the main thing. It was cold, wet, and dark outside but somehow, the house had a radiance about it and I started unpacking, wondering where everything went. Not being used to rustling around in my wife's underwear draw it had suddenly become of immense interest, out of necessity, where she kept everything, and where I was going to find things in the future. We had our evening meal and then went to the hospital to see how Helen was doing. She managed to recognise Mavis, which I think, did them both good and then she returned to her deep slumbers. We traced a doctor who only told us what we already knew, she was stable but anything could happen over the next few weeks.

Mavis was now tired and so it was time to return home and go to bed. We had never tried the transfers up the stairs before so if it did not work I assured Mavis that she would be taken back to the hospital and I would personally beg for her bed back. Mavis took the wheelchair into the hall and I positioned the ramps over the three stairs. It was tight and I had to spend some time adjusting them so that they fitted the track of the wheelchair. Mavis very gingerly aligned the chair and started to climb up the ramps. The two front wheels rose quite easily but when the rear drive wheels contacted with the comparatively smooth surface they started to slip and the chair stayed at the bottom. I asked Mavis to take the chair back again and instead of trying slowly to take it faster and see if the extra momentum could gain any further progress. She tried again but it still did not work so we had great wheel spinning on the ramp but no further progress. I concluded that the ramps were too steep for the weight on the chair and therefore Mavis has to reverse off the ramp again so that I could do some re thinking.

Finding a tape measure, I measured all the ramps that Bill and I had made earlier to allow Mavis to get into the house. One of the smaller ones seemed to be about the correct length. I carried it in and re-measured it all out again. It certainly helped the ramps ratio, as the incline was now much less. The only major drawback was that now, instead of the ramps 'resting' on the stairs, they made a bridge between the end of the wooden ramp and the top stair. This left a two foot gap underneath at the highest point. Providing Mavis could keep steering the chair on the two ramps we did not have a problem. However if the chair did come off the ramps for any reason then she had a long fall. There is nothing like fear to focus the mind! Mavis reversed the chair to the end of the hall, which meant the back was as close to the front door as she could get it. I put the wooden ramp back down and then put the two ramps between the wooden one and the top stair. Leaving as much overhang as I could between the two lots of ramps, Mavis slowly trundled her way forwards. Whilst she was on the wooden ramp all was fine. However when she started to go over the 'bridge' she announced it felt a little strange. "Was everything looking Ok"? I went to the side and noticed that the combined weight was now making the ramps bend a little in the middle, but I assured her that the specification on the ramps said that they should be able to take a load of 25 stone. My calculations showed 24.6 stone so that should be fine and anyway, I was sure that the ramp manufacturers factored in a margin of error. She kept going very tentatively while I held my breath and after what seemed an eternity she made it to the top step. The only problem now was that it was extremely tight trying to get enough room for myself as well as the chair to accomplish the manoeuvre from the chair to the stair lift. I reversed the chair back a little, which left it half on the ramps and half on the stair, and lifted Mavis to the standing position and we started to make the turn to the stair lift.

All would have been fine if my bottom had not knocked against the joystick of the wheelchair. This put it into silly mode and it attempted to do a 90o turn and fall of the ramps. Ok; so lesson one learnt; switch the wheelchair off when in the correct place. After the initial shock to both of us, Mavis got her bum onto the seat of the stair lift and I rescued the wheelchair. After that, it was up to the top of the stairs to make the transfer from the stair lift to the manual chair. This went amazingly well as the thought of us both falling down the full flight of stairs, if we made a mistake, did not appeal to either of us. Mavis was then wheeled to the bathroom so that I could wash her ready for bed. Dressed in her nightdress I wheeled her into our bedroom, she was then able to see for the first time how her bed looked being mounted on some 24 bricks, and she wondered if it would take her weight. I jumped onto the bed to prove the point, and after some minor adjustments, we climbed into bed.

The tension and emotions are hard to communicate. There was a time I did not believe it possible that this would ever happen again and yet I had continued to pray that it would. We lay there and talked a little and I found out how things were changed. Mavis could now sleep only on her back, as she could not turn over at all. I think she was wondering what I was doing when I started to touch various parts of her body, one after another, to ascertain that no, it wasn't just me, but Mavis's left arm and left leg were absolutely freezing whereas the rest of her body was at normal temperature. Unfortunately for me, she slept on the right side of the bed so that the cold side of her body would always be against me. It did not look as if I could rely on her any more to help keep me warm in bed. Instead, it looked as if the roles were going to be reversed in future. Mavis had not realised before that this was happening, so I made a note of reporting it to the Doctor next time we saw him.

I only seemed to have been asleep for a little while when Mavis awoke me to say she needed to go to the toilet. I got up and moved quickly around to her side of the bed. I lifted her from the bed to the wheelchair and from the wheelchair to the toilet. Business done a complete reversal of operations and we were back into a rather cold bed. I do not think it had occurred to me before how cold a bed can get if both occupants vacate it together. Usually only one person gets up at a time, if at all, so the bed still stays warm. Still, I tried to go back to sleep now, hopefully, until the morning. It was not to be however, and I do not know why. Perhaps it was because Mavis was feeling vulnerable, or perhaps she was afraid of not being able to get to the toilet in time, but for whatever reason we repeated the performance of getting up and going to the toilet and then back into a cold bed a further six times. I could not believe it! Every time I just went back to sleep, I was woken again, and by 07:00 I was wondering why I had been so keen to have Mavis home.

Tuesday 16th November 2004.

We were both tired and I was probably grumpy however, there seemed little point in keep returning to bed so after the last visit we decided we might as well stay up. We also had other exciting things to achieve today. I took Mavis's nightdress off and she stood so that I could sit her on the bath board. I lifted her legs one at a time into the bath and she was now ready for her first home shower. I tried tucking the shower curtain in around her and switched on the shower. Now whether it was because I was tired or not I do not know, but I agree that forgetting to move the showerhead so that the first lot of cold water did not go all over Mavis was unforgivable. It did start to warm up though and after much screaming Mavis started to enjoy her first home shower for nearly six months. Not really knowing exactly what I was doing I just washed her all over; I washed her hair and then dried her in situ. Then, taking one leg out at a time I managed to get Mavis dangling over the edge of the bath ready to be dressed. To make sure she was dry I covered her completely in Talcum powder. I then attempted to dress her, which proved to be a lot more difficult that it would have first seemed. To start with, I am far more used to taking Bra's off than putting them on. It was just very unfortunate that I had managed to pick a clean bra that was very plain and therefore it did not give many clues as to which was the inside and therefore which was the out. After a great deal of manoeuvring I only realised that things were not right when it became obvious that the clips at the back usually had the hooks going into the eyes and not the other way round. We had a good laugh at my incompetence and then moved to putting on socks.

This was a real revelation. Putting them on the good right foot was easy but trying to put them onto the left was almost impossible. When you are dressing children there is generally a resistance that you can push against, giving you control to move the sock up the foot. When the leg and foot just hang there if you push the sock onto the foot it just moves away and if you push more it just moves away further. We succeeded in the end by me sitting on the floor with my right leg wrapped around Mavis's left leg, so stopping it moving away. Therefore, before we knew it, it was 10:30, and all we had accomplished was to get Mavis out of bed, showered and half dressed. It has taken some 3½ hours, but what a learning curve! I rang 'S' the hospital OT and asked her if we could have another commode as this would save me having to take the one that they had already supplied up and down the stairs every night and this she agreed to. She asked how the first night had gone. I did not tell her that I was already thinking I had made the wrong decision in bringing Mavis home. We now had to try to reverse last night's performance and go downstairs.

We transferred from the manual chair to the stair lift and then down for the transfer to the electric chair on the landing. As Mavis stayed on the stair lift, I put the ramps back together and once into the wheelchair I attempted to drive it up the ramps. Fortunately, it was me and not Mavis driving and I can only assume it was because I was going a little bit faster. I noticed that one of the ramps was beginning to move. Instead of the wheelchair going up the ramp, it was moving the ramp backwards. I gingerly lowered the chair back to the hall again and got my drill. I drilled a hole into the wooden ramp and then one each into the fibreglass ramps.

I then put a small nut and bolt into the fibreglass ramps that could now act like a location pin to the wooden one. Now it worked. Nearly twelve noon and Mavis had not even had her breakfast, if she had still been in hospital she would have been preparing ready to have her lunch.

Mavis, having descended from the stair lift to her wheelchair, now wanted to visit the toilet again. We had arranged with 'S' the hospital OT, that until the extension was built we would be able to manage with a commode in the cupboard under the stairs. We were now going to find out if this worked. It was clear that space was tight, once Mavis was sitting on the commode inside the cupboard it was apparent that it was so tight that the door would not close. Fortunately, we were not overlooked by anyone so the door could be left open with the window curtains just slightly pulled to preserve Mavis' modesty should anyone purposely look in.

In the afternoon, we visited Helen again and had our first experience of using the disabled toilet in the hospital. When we eventually found one, it had a notice on it saying that if you needed to use it you had to obtain a code for the lock from reception. It was now another two minutes to reception, a wait in the queue there for the code and then another two minutes back to the toilet. Due to the delay, as soon as we entered the toilet, it was too late and Mavis had wet herself. Thank goodness again for the electric hand dryers and nobody else desperate to use this toilet. Helen was still looking poorly but all the staff, once you found them, seemed to think she was Ok, so we came home and I made dinner. I asked Mavis what she wanted and surprise.......... "Anything with chips." Still as it was her first proper day at home, I supposed I could indulge her a little. After a dinner of egg and chips, and a little television, it was time for bed again. Not that I was looking forward to it, I wasn't. Mavis wheeled the chair as close to the front door as it would go and I put the ramps down, this time locating the end of the screw into the hole on the wooden ramp. Mavis drove the wheelchair up as if she had been doing it all her life and we were in bed within ¾ of an hour. I dropped off to sleep and yet again after what only seemed to be a very short time I heard "Michael can you get me up I need the toilet again". Pointing out that it was only two hours since she had been did not seem to have any effect and therefore it was all the rigours of bed to wheelchair, to toilet and back again.

What amazed me was the amount of urine she actually managed to pass and I was very thankful that I had taken her. I concluded that women must have two bladders instead of the one apportioned to males. These are used at a completely different time to each other except at night when both are brought into play to cause maximum disruption. So why do they call it "old men's syndrome"? We went back to sleep and I waited for the next sleep intrusion. When it did come, I was just about to say "you can't need to go again already" when I noticed the clock said 07:50 so I could not complain and roused myself ready to fight another day.

Wednesday 17th November 2004.

'V' the social worker was calling to see us today. Thank goodness she said it was going to be in the afternoon. Preparing Mavis for the day, toileting, showering and then dressing seemed to be taking all the morning and she did not really spend that long on the toilet. I put it down to the amount of time deciding which way her bra was to go on and felt that if this was not going to improve then I was fighting a losing battle.

'V' arrived, this time with her boss, and we went through everything that had happened over the last two days. Her boss inspected the house and questioned exactly what the council were going to do. She remarked that our little kitchen was not going to make a suitable one for a wheelchair user. For the first time I realised that this was another modification that needed planning for. I had assumed that because I was going to do all the cooking, then the kitchen would become my domain and therefore did not need altering. However, after talking it through with 'V' and her colleague it became apparent that if Mavis was going to improve even just a little, then she might be able to do a few things for herself. I therefore had to bear this in mind for the future.

Bedtime soon came around again and we went through the ritual of placing out the ramps and worked the system well this time so we were soon in bed. This was a lot earlier than I would normally retire but I was that tired I was actually looking forward to it. I have to admit that getting used to Mavis being back in bed again was proving difficult. Before the stroke we had always slept in the spoons position but now, because Mavis could only sleep on her back, finding out where to put your arms and legs so that both parties would be comfortable involved a great deal of trial and error.

Thursday 18th November 2004.

Only two visits to the toilet overnight and because we went to bed so early, I awoke to feel a little more able to cope. It still took nearly three hours showering and pampering Mavis, ready to go downstairs, but since there was little else to do that needed urgent attention, I quickly realised that in reality it did not matter how long things took. We went back to see Helen, but again very little change in her condition. Her bed though could have been cleaner and as I sat there at her bedside, looking at the other very frail and feeble geriatrics on the ward, I began to wonder why in Gods eternal plan he had allowed such a terrible thing as the indignity that goes with old age. When we arrived home, we decided to cheer ourselves up and invited Bill and Pat along for supper. I think for the first time since all this happened it became remarkably clear that if anything needed to be done it was me that had to do it.

Mavis and I had always helped each other in the past. All through our marriage, we had always worked as a team, when we could. Now I had lost the most important member of the team and in the future would have to do everything by myself. Not that I minded, I didn't, it just came as a bit of a revelation. By nine o'clock Mavis's eyes were beginning to droop and she asked Bill and Pat if they would go home as she was tired. This really surprised me a) that she had been so frank and b) she had become so tired so quickly. They left and I put Mavis to bed and came downstairs again to clear up. By the time I was upstairs again she was sound asleep. I just stood there and watched her for what seemed ages, just as you do with your children, wondering just what the future held in store for both of us.

Friday 19th November 2004.

We arrived downstairs at now what was becoming our usual time of 11:45 and after having breakfast (or lunch) I started to tidy up all the deposits that had accumulated in the room since the beginning of the week. On Mavis's release from hospital, they had given me a copy of her care plan. I decided to read it through to her. It upset her terribly, not that she wanted me to stop reading but I think much of it were things that she had no recollection of. Just hearing about what went on in the hospital was quite a revealing experience for her.

Saturday 20th November 2004.

We are now beginning to settle into a routine and the day passes in exactly the same way the rest of the week had done. Up, showered and dressed, then downstairs, usually by lunchtime and then to the hospital in the afternoon to see Helen. After this it was back home, something to eat and then after a short time, bed. Tomorrow was going to be different though as we had to be at church for 10:30 - and not when we managed to get there. Working on the fact that it had taken us at least 3 ½ hours to prepare for each day during the week and that we needed some time to drive there I set the alarm for 06:30 and waited to see what tomorrow would bring. If nothing else it would give us some practice for Monday when Mavis started her outpatient physiotherapy, for that we had to be at the hospital also for 10:30.

Sunday 21st November 2004.

The alarm went off and I was as delighted as a new parent whose child had just slept through the night. How wonderful was that, a whole night's sleep without having to leave a warm bed to face the cold and then not being able to go back to sleep again. It seemed an early start but we needed every moment of it. We managed to leave the house at 10:10. I had however, forgotten to allow the extra time to unload the wheelchair at church and transfer Mavis inside. They were already into the service when we arrived. Never mind we had made it. Whereas in the past 10:30 on a Sunday morning still seemed early, it now seemed as if we were already half way through the day and it should have been lunchtime. Whilst pre ambulating these thoughts, I suddenly realised I had not thought about Sunday dinner. Planning for food was going to prove the most difficult part of my integration into our new life and I was just hoping we had something in the freezer that would suffice. After exchanging all the pleasantries at the end of the service we went home. Fortunately, I was able to find some ready meals in the freezer, still left over from when Helen used to cater for herself some weekends when Mavis and I were away. I must admit they made quite a good meal considering their sell by date.

We went back to church for the evening service and eventually returned home again at 20:00. We were both tired after such a long day. I made tea and we both decided it was bedtime and an early night was

111

called for. I got the ramps out and Mavis aimed the wheelchair as usual. Now I do not know whether it was because Mavis was exceptionally tired or not, but instead of the chair going up the ramps as before, the front wheels were steered over the edge of the ramps, about halfway up. Mavis was now suspended, with half the chair on the ramps and half hanging perilously over the edge with a two-foot drop below. Fortunately, she had stopped in time, however, it did bring home to me how much danger I was putting Mavis in each day until the house was sufficiently modified to enable Mavis to sleep down stairs. I helped to balance the chair on the ramps and very slowly, Mavis reversed it down to the bottom again and so she survived to try again. This time she missed the bottom of the ramps completely and they came crashing down the steps. If this was going to keep happening, we were never going to get to bed. After rebuilding the ramps, I took over the controls and we managed to steer Mavis upstairs to bed. By this time, there were tears everywhere. I did not know if this was because she had been so scared on the ramps or because she was just extremely tired. We both climbed into bed shattered and I set the alarm for 06:30 the following morning.

Monday 22nd November 2004.

Perhaps tiring Mavis out totally was the way to ensure a good night's sleep as she managed another whole night right the way through. Therefore, after showering, dressing and breakfast it was now to the hospital for Mavis's physio. I wheeled her into a room neither of us had been in before, even though it was the same hospital that Mavis had been discharged from last week. We were introduced to a new physio called 'C' who made it very clear from the outset that she was going to do her best for Mavis. We went through all Mavis's history and of course, we heard yet again the dreaded question "so what would you like to achieve Mavis." Now since I was doing most of the answering, because Mavis was finding it extremely difficult to find any of the correct words this morning, I decided to enquire if 'C' had a sense of humour or not by replying "We would like to achieve no 23 in the Karma Sutra" and I said it with a dead straight face. 'C' looked at Mavis, but I think Mavis had not quite heard what I had said and therefore managed also to keep her face straight. 'C' then looked at me again so I thought, as it was our first contact time, I would put her out of her disbelief. I said, "We couldn't do it before Mavis had her stroke but it is something we would like to now achieve" She took it well and it was going to be the start of a close relationship that was going to last over a year.

The first ten minutes of the session were spent appraising exactly what Mavis could do rather than the things she could not. At the end 'C' announced that Mavis was going to work as she had never worked before to see what could be achieved. I immediately warmed to this girl and so started in earnest Mavis trying to stand. After 30 minutes, Mavis was crying but had to admit that the session had gone very well. She had taken two steps with our help, so it was a start. We left with Mavis feeling apprehensive about what lay in front of her and me happy because at last we had come across someone who was thinking positively, irrespective of whether Mavis liked it or not. The next appointment was for Wednesday at the same time and so we went home, Mavis totally exhausted.

Tuesday 23rd November 2004.

At least we could sleep in this morning but the call of Mavis's bladder came at about 7:15 so it was nearly time to get up anyway. 'P' the guy from the council arrived to show us the plans he was proposing for the extension, and although they were Ok neither he nor I were really satisfied with them. They fitted the purpose but they did not really fit in with the rest of the house somehow. Unable to think of a better way, reluctantly I agreed and he said he would pass them to an architect to have them drawn up properly for approval. Apart from this visit, Mavis seemed to sleep in her chair all day so it allowed time for me to catch up on some housework.

Wednesday 24th November 2004.

Up early again and down to the hospital. As before 'C' really put Mavis through her paces (literally). I could see that although it is extremely hard work for Mavis, between 'C' and herself if anything is going to happen then they will make sure it does. We returned home and I had decided that we have to do something about our banking situation. As nearly all our married life I had been in a job that necessitated me working away from home for at least some of the week, Mavis had always looked after the money. It had been convenient and over the years she had opened accounts in both her name only or joint ones that enabled me to access our money if ever I needed to. This was now becoming a millstone around my neck. For instance, Mavis had a separate current account through which she used to pay some standing orders. The bank would not let me near it and therefore, if sometimes it went overdrawn, then it had high amounts of Bank charges added to it. On one occasion, I had to literally take Mavis from the hospital to the Bank just to have things sorted and then take her back again. All the usual banking had been accessed under a joint account where Mavis used the telephone banking system to do the necessary. Now she could not. She could not remember anything to do with the account, the passwords, or even how to implement them. To be honest about it, even if she could have remembered, her dysphasia would not let her say the numbers aloud quickly enough. I thought I would try using Mavis's access, but once they realised I was not Mavis they would not talk to me. They would only talk to her and she could not talk to them. What a wasted afternoon and Mavis just wanted to sleep.

Thursday 25th November 2004.

Today bladder timings have worked in our favour for once. A trip at 03:00 and another at 06:30 then back to bed, as today there was nothing to get up for. I awoke and looked at the clock …10:20 gosh it felt good. We decided to dispense with the shower this morning and this allowed us to catch up a bit of time. Breakfast was now at the normal time of 12:15. The lady from the grant's department of the council came to means test us this afternoon and after all the preliminaries we were faced with some hard facts. This extension was going to cost a lot of money and they expected Mavis and I to pay a large amount of it ourselves. It appeared that the grant towards extensions is usually capped at £25,000 and the plan put forward (under 'P') was going to be nearer the £40,000 mark. We discussed this at great length as I considered it unfair to expect us to contribute to a design I did not want and one that was really imposed on us, taking preference over the one that I had worked out previously using the through floor lift. She accepted this and having taken all our financial details left saying she would consult with 'P' again. However if we were not prepared to pay the extra £15,000 she did not know what would happen or whether the extension would be built at all. We sank back into the chairs after she had departed knowing we had another battle on our hands, but life seemed to be one constant battle these days. Perhaps as I am getting older I am just getting a little bit grumpier.

Friday 26th November 2004.

Mavis has begun to settle down now and life is good. One stop to the loo overnight is great and I have recovered most of my lost sleep. After breakfast, we went to the hospital to see Helen who is still unwell but apparently no worse, so something to be thankful for. On the way home, I made the mistake of again asking Mavis what she would like for the evening meal. "Anything nice with chips" eventually came out amongst all the Dysphasia so as a treat we called in for Pizza and chips and took it home to have a nice evening in front of the television together.

Sunday 28th November 2004.

Whilst we were at church this morning, Mel called us over to say could we see him after the service as he may have something for us. We found him later and he took us to a small room where he showed us a strange looking machine. He explained that he had been given (I didn't ask why) this motorised lifter that can raise and lower people into the bath and did we want it? I studied it carefully and decided that if nothing else it was worth having a go. With grateful thanks, we took it home with us determined to try it as soon as I could work out how it operated.

Monday 29th November 2004.

Up really early this morning as it was back for physiotherapy. I did not think today was the best day to start finding out how the bathing machine worked. After a quick shower and breakfast, we arrived at our appointment. This girl really makes Mavis work and will not take "No" or "I can't" for an answer. I could not see any blood, but the sweat and the tears were definitely to be found in abundance.

We drove from one hospital to the next to see Helen and noticed that she was now sitting up in bed and looking a bit more with it. Long visiting times seemed to tire them both, so after about 45 minutes we left to come home. I transferred Mavis to a comfortable chair from the wheelchair and went to make a cup of coffee. By the time I returned she was fast asleep. Whilst she was sleeping, I found the bathing machine, assembled it together, and put it on to charge the batteries. I could now see how it worked, but because it had no instruction manual with it, there was no indication what load it could or would take. If we did use it, it was going to be another big gamble.

Tuesday 30th November 2004.

Despite the afternoon 'nap' yesterday Mavis still managed to sleep most of the night with only one loo stop, so all was well. I asked her if she wanted to try a bath today, as it was our only 'clear' day. With great apprehension, she agreed. I ran a nice warm bath and found some ancient bath things to put into the water to make it smell nice and inviting. I lowered the machine into the bath raising the seat as high as it would go so that Mavis could sit on it. The seat did swivel to allow for easy access and so I managed to get Mavis on the seat. So far so good. It was only when I let go that the machine toppled to the side. Mavis was left petrified that she was going to topple over into the bath, and so was I as the thought of trying to recover the situation filled me with great apprehension. I heaved Mavis back into the upright position again and lifted her off the machine and onto the side of the bath.

In examining what had gone wrong, it was clear that we had somehow managed to dislodge two of the suckers that held the machine steady onto the bottom of the bath. Once rectified, I persuaded Mavis that we should have another try. At last, she was seated correctly on the seat of the machine. I then pressed the control and Mavis slowly descended into the bath to be virtually covered by bubbles. I topped the water up so that it became warm again and Mavis sat there crying. I did not know why she was crying but it seemed to happen all the time now and it was hard to become used to this reaction every time it happened. Trying to ask why didn't help either, as whatever the emotion was that caused her to cry also affected her dysphasia. Extracting an answer at the time was almost impossible.

Now all clean and smelly it was then time to get Mavis out. I had assumed that because I had charged the battery overnight it would be fully charged and it's fair to say I still can't be sure if it was because the battery didn't hold its full charge any more or because Mavis was too heavy for the machine. However, just as I pressed the button to start raising Mavis up, the battery low light came on and the chair Mavis was sitting on became slower and slower. It eventually came to a complete stop about 4 inches from the top of the bath and so we were stuck. What do we do now? We discussed various options but in the end, I drained the water from the bath, wrapping Mavis in towels so she did not become cold. I took the battery out and gave it a quick 5-minute charge hoping that it would be enough to allow her to reach the top and it did, just! Dried and dressed it was now 11:55, just in time for breakfast.

Down to the hospital to see Helen, then back again to get the evening meal ready. There did not seem to be much time left over in the day to do all the other things that needed doing like washing, ironing and cleaning or even some work.

Wednesday 1st December 2004.

Up early again this morning for Mavis's next appointment with the physio. As soon as we arrived in the department, she had Mavis from the wheelchair and standing. She went through Mavis's posture like a regimental sergeant major. Within minutes, Mavis had tears running down her cheeks and I was very pleased that 'C' took very little notice. At the end of the session we explored what had happened, why Mavis had been crying and why 'C' had ignored her. We left happy. As we drove home, Mavis and I discussed the session at great length and Mavis agreed that although she cried she had enjoyed the session and thought that this was what she needed if she was going to accomplish anything in the future. By the time we reached home, the postman had been and there was a letter from the council. It explained that under the circumstances, they were prepared to find the extra money to fund the whole of the extension and therefore the project would be going ahead after all. Enclosed was a contract between the council and ourselves where we agreed that 'P' would undertake the project manager's role and make sure everything was done properly.

The next thing to do was to have the plans drawn up properly so that we could apply for planning permission. Mavis sat there crying again but could not tell me why. I was beginning to realise that I was going to need all the patience I could muster to come to terms with the fact that the stroke had obviously moved Mavis's bladder closer to her eyeballs.

Thursday 2nd December 2004.

Another early rise, but this time it was back to the hospital to see the speech therapist. As it was in the outpatients department in the main hospital, I knew it might be difficult to find somewhere to park and I was not disappointed. After searching for a parking place for some twenty minutes, I gave up and eventually found somewhere nearly 15 minutes walk away from the hospital. It was raining hard but I did not have time to take the cycle capes from the car. With Mavis holding an umbrella over herself the best she could, I ran pushing her in the wheelchair back into the hospital. If ever you have done this before, you quickly realise that unless the pusher is over 6 feet tall, you cannot see over someone in a wheelchair who is carrying an umbrella, so navigation was a bit fraught.

We arrived just in time, both looking wet and bedraggled to be introduced to a petite Asian looking lady who was the speech therapist. Now I know that everyone has to make an assessment but this session was so boring I felt myself dropping off to sleep. Had it not been for the fact that I was keen to know what was happening and why, I probably would have. She gave Mavis various pictures to look at and Mavis was surprisingly good at answering them. She scored 98 out of 100 for the first test. After this, the lady asked the standard question and getting a very stern look from Mavis I realised that No.23 from the Karma Sutra is not to pass my lips. Mavis replied that she had great difficulty answering or speaking on the telephone so it was agreed that next week Mavis would be given some practical help to do this. Little did we know what we were to encounter then.

Friday 3rd December 2004.

Up early again to reach the hospital for yet another physio session. Today 'C' made Mavis sit on her bench that has been elevated and had her sitting, standing and sitting again, then right at the end we both supported Mavis to enable her to take a couple of steps on her own. We came away elated that Mavis had been able to do this and 'C's no nonsense approach was beginning work. We then went on to see Helen who, today had managed, with the aid of a Zimmer, to take herself to the toilet on her own. Without the nurse's knowledge she had locked herself in and was unable to turn back the lock. Eventually they did miss her and after a long search located her. We now had to tell her that in future she must only go anywhere with a nurse. While we were talking, I noticed that Helen had a white tongue, but presumed it was the aftermath of having just taken some medicine. I thought very little of it at the time.

Saturday 4th December 2004.

The week had taken its toll on Mavis as apart from rising for bladder relief has she slept until nearly midday. It was much like having a baby.

You know she needed her sleep but you wanted to go to wake her up to make sure she was all right. Today I did the washing and decided that since it was such a nice day, I would wash all the dusters as well. Nobody ever told me that nice fairly new yellow dusters have a propensity for losing their colour. I had to break the news to Mavis when she woke up that all her underwear was now a rather nice primrose colour, apart from her two bras' that were now more a dirty grey. I must remember that in future.

Monday 6th December 2004.

Back to the hospital for more physio. 'C' is good for Mavis. She ignored the tears and tried to push Mavis further than she thinks she can go; and succeeds. We saw Mavis sitting and rising albeit from a very high adjustable bed but each movement brought about a little more confidence and therefore a little more trust in the fact that her leg would now support her. We took a few more steps and by this time Mavis was completely exhausted but never mind, she was still improving.

Tuesday 7th December 2004.

I suddenly realised that Christmas was not too far away and this year everything was going to be left up to me. Hopefully, with a little input from Mavis, we could start on the long haul of presents and cards. We had a visit from this woman who runs the Sunderland Stroke club as Mavis had been referred to her, presumably by the hospital. She was very officious and seemed to think that we ought to jump at the chance of Mavis going to one of her placements, "as they were very limited". We insisted that Mavis and I needed to talk about it a lot before making any decisions as I could see many complications. She left, I think feeling a little frustrated. I could not help thinking she would make a very good double-glazing or second hand car sales person.

Mavis and I continued to discuss it in detail and whilst I could see all the benefits for Mavis, it had its drawbacks. Not the least was that at the club, there would be no one to help Mavis go to the toilet and she cannot go by herself. I would therefore need to go with her all the time but I was not allowed into the room with the "clients". The carers had to wait in the hall outside. This did not seem a good use of my time but, if Mavis really wanted to go, I would do it. Mavis was not really too keen though. She was worried about being in an outside environment by herself and in all honesty, I really did not think she was ready for coping with it yet. We decided to let the opportunity pass. As it transpires, the amount of physio that Mavis has lined up for her means that it would be very seldom that we would be able to go anyway.

Wednesday 8th December 2004.

Every day we had visited Helen I had noticed that her tongue was becoming whiter, so I decided to hunt out the doctors concerned. About an hour later, I managed to find one with enough time to talk to me and he informed me that Helen was suffering from Thrush. Seeing my total surprise he explained to me that you can get it in the throat as well as the genitals and it is usually caused by the antibiotics taking away all the body's natural defence mechanisms. The laughable thing was that they were treating this with another antibiotic, and so I wondered what other medical conditions she might develop later on.

Back at home, I still have not fully resolved the banking situation. Red tape and more Red tape, so this afternoon I decided to sort it out for the last time. I had to take Mavis to her banks so that they could put me on all the accounts and I spent the rest of the day setting up Internet banking. The main problem with this of course is that if anything happens to me, Mavis will be in an even worse position, as she cannot use the computer or the Internet, let alone remember all the passwords required. Let us hope I stay healthy for a good long time.

Thursday 9th December 2004.

This morning we returned to see the speech therapist again and she confirmed that she is going to help Mavis use the telephone. I am not sure what I expected but I certainly did not expect the girl to spend half an hour showing Mavis how to pick the telephone up from the receiver and replacing it. Mavis knew what a telephone was and how to use it mechanically. We were both hoping that perhaps there was some tried and tested method for overcoming the trouble of finding the right words to use on the telephone. After 30 minutes, my patience had expired and so I tried to explain to the girl, as nicely as I could, that I thought this exercise was a complete waste of time, including hers. This did not go down at all well and she informed us that the lesson was finished and she would try to think up something more practical for the next lesson. We both looked forward to it.

Friday 10th December 2004.

Back to physio. It is just as well I work from home as I could never do a "proper job" working from an office or such, there was never enough time in the day just looking after Mavis and all the visits to the various outpatient departments, let alone go to work. We could however see results from the physio. Each time we went Mavis stood for a little longer, walked another tentative step further and managed to rise from a little lower down, so things are definitely improving.

Saturday 11th December 2004.

This morning saw the arrival of the new three-piece suite. Why is it that whenever you buy things in shops they always seem so small yet at home in the room, they seem so much larger. I was worried that the men would not be able to manoeuvre it through the door but, experts that they were, after a couple of attempts in it came and was duly unpacked and assembled. As soon as the men had gone, I transferred Mavis from the wheelchair to the settee and she tried to stand up on her own. It took a tremendous amount of effort but with a little bit of coaxing from me (a small bar of chocolate just out of reach) she eventually managed and we agreed the purchase to be a success. The only problem now was how to dispose of the old suite, but that was for another day. We went to see Helen, to tell her the news, and her tongue had regained a little more of its pinkness. She told us that a physio had come to see her yesterday after our visit, telling her he was going to get her walking with a 'Zimmer' frame with wheels on. Perhaps it is my sense of humour, but it did conjure up a vision of Helen gliding up and down the ward in a 'Denis the Menace' T-shirt scaring everyone back into their beds. I just smiled and told her that she would do well.

Monday 13th December 2004.

Back on the treadmill. We go to hospital one for physio, then hospital two, to see Helen and then home. I was really tired, let alone Mavis, but it did seem to be worth it. Both Mavis and Helen were improving and it looked as if Helen would be home for Christmas, so that would be good.

Tuesday 14th December 2004.

We went to see Helen as usual and I asked her if her Zimmer had arrived. It seemed it had but it was so big that she could not use it. The physio had promised to take it away and return with a smaller one. When we arrived home, it was clear that I still had to do something with the old three-piece suite. It was light and so I could just about lift it on my own. What I could not do was manoeuvre it through the doors and even if I could, it was doubtful if I could get it into the estate. Once again, it registered, and I had to accept that my 'mate' over the last 36 years, was not able to give me a hand. It was obvious, how could she? Yet, it had just sunk in that from now on it had to be just one person doing everything. Either anything I could not manage on my own I had to 'borrow' a neighbour for, or it would not be done. Therefore, in this case the solution was simple. I would simply cut it up into manageable pieces, which would make it easier to transport to the skip. I did not realise just how much dust it would create. However, within half an hour, the three pieces were cut into a manageable carrying size and Mavis was covered in sawdust.

Wednesday 15th December 2004.

Back to physio. Mavis did really well and walked nearly thirty paces with much goading from the physio and myself. We left that hospital and went to the other to see Helen and she has had another setback, probably pneumonia. It does not look as if she will be coming home for Christmas after all

Thursday 16th December 2004.

We are back to the hospital for the speech therapy class at 10:00. So up early again. Mavis only needed to rise once during the night so at least we both had a decent night's sleep. This lesson was a little better thought out. She tried to persuade Mavis to say what she wanted to say repeatedly until she was confident with it before she picked up the telephone. This worked fine of course until the person on the other end said something that you have not rehearsed for. Back came the silence or the stuttering/word fishing from Mavis. Not a lot gained there then. The lady then embarked on a series of other tests of which Mavis only managed 98% correct and I queried the other two percentages. It seemed the question was which one was the odd one out of three birds and why? I asked the speech therapist if she could answer the question. She told me which one she thought it might be but couldn't back it up with any reasoning, so I then offered an alternative and gave what I thought was a fairly compelling reason why I was right. We discussed this in some depth and I convinced her that any one of all three answers could have been right. As such, it was very unfair to mark anyone as being wrong, when really they could have been right. She awarded Mavis the extra points and we left, but I do not think the therapist was happy. The next lesson was set for the New Year.

We must get the Christmas shopping finished so it is off to the Metro Centre. I parked the car and transferred Mavis into the lightweight transfer chair, as the electric one will not be so easy to manage in the shops. What an experience. People just do not seem to be aware of anyone or anything else around them. I think I only managed to hit two people or more accurately, they walked into us. Waiting to get close to a counter so that Mavis could see what she wanted was always marred by someone pushing in front of us so by 16:00 we had both had enough. We came home; I made tea and by 21:00, we were both in bed.

Friday 17th December 2004.

Back to physio and then across to Ailsa's as we have agreed to baby-sit Henry, our grandson. This is another new experience (no not the baby-sitting) as we will be sleeping downstairs on a bed settee using the commode. Mavis is a little apprehensive as to how we will manage. As it turned out, it was very similar to the way we managed at home, so everything passed well. We might even try to do it again someday.

Saturday 18th December 2004.

Henry usually goes to drama classes on a Saturday. As both his parents were probably still the worse for wear from the previous night, we agreed to take him. He managed to tell us where it was and we alighted from the car, parking close to the building. We slowly walked from the car to the bottom of the staircase in what used to be an old mill of a building. We were then confronted with three flights of stairs just to reach the first floor. This was going to be quite some undertaking for Mavis as she had only walked up two or three steps before, let alone three flights. I told her if she could walk up one step, then she was capable of walking up many, as the sequence was the same, just being repeated more often. With great resolve and determination, we started, with Mavis having an arm around my neck and Henry pushing from behind. Now it might have taken nearly 15 minutes with a breather on the landings in between flights, but we eventually made it. We had floods of tears at the top, which I was not sure if they were due to exhaustion or triumph. Putting those aside we delivered Henry to his class then went farther down the corridor to avail ourselves of a hot chocolate in the coffee shop. After drinking her chocolate Mavis dropped off to sleep so I put the tears down to exhaustion, probably both mental and physical, but we had triumphed over another obstacle and that was good.

Sunday 19th December 2004.

We were up early and went to church with Ailsa, Mark, and Henry. The congregation met Mavis very warmly and we had more tears. I think this time they are just emotional tears so they were ignored. Now we had not realised it but it was communion this morning and, being Church of England, everyone goes to the rail at the front of the altar. This was a reasonable walk and had a few steps involved. If Mavis could walk up so many steps yesterday then this was going to be a cinch for her today. When our turn came, we rose and arrived quite easily at the rail for communion. It was on the way back that I noticed Karen, one of Ailsa's friends, crying in the pew but at the time could not ask why. At the end of the service, Karen came over to us and explained that her tears were of thanksgiving and joy. She had seen Mavis do something that even three months ago nobody had dreamt that she would ever accomplish. Funny thing women and their tears.

We had lunch, played a couple of games with Henry in the afternoon, and after tea returned home. I must admit I was shattered when we eventually climbed into our own bed. We men are not used to multitasking, I think having to think for both Mavis and myself, as well as having physically to look after Mavis and Henry for some of the time was just a little challenging for me. Still this weekend had been a landmark. It was another little accomplishment into returning to near normal life again and it had gone very well indeed.

Monday 20th December 2004.

As Mavis managed to use the stairs over the weekend, we decide that she can attempt to use the stairs at home as well. We tried the three stairs to the chair lift in the same manner as Saturday but without Henry pushing, and it is so successful that we can now dispense with the nightly excitement of steering the electric wheel chair up the ramps. If I fit a banister rail on both sides of the stairs Mavis might even be able to manage it by herself.

Apart from the usual treadmill of back and forth to the hospital, either for physio, or to see Helen, the rest of the week passed quietly and without incident. The good news was that Helen was well enough to come out of hospital for Christmas Day.

Saturday 25th December 2004.

Ailsa had invited us all to go to hers for Christmas Day and so it was to be. Mavis and I arose early and after making Mavis ready, we took the car down to the hospital to collect Helen. I was a little disappointed to note when I arrived that Helen was not ready. I wondered if she had had another setback and she could not come out, but no, it was just that the staff had not got around to getting her ready. All the elderly people in the ward had been given a present "from Santa" and so the next hour was filled either getting Helen ready or being shown for the umpteenth time, her makeup bag from Santa. It was just after 11:15 when I wheeled Helen to the car and I attempted to load her into the back seat. Her legs would not support her and after a few attempts, we decided that Mavis would sit in the back and I would lift Helen into the front, as there was more room. This was accomplished and at about 11:30 I drove out of Sunderland with my two charges to arrive in Carlisle just in time for lunch.

I lifted Helen out of the car and carried her into the house where I thought she might be able to walk again but she couldn't. To this day, we don't really know why, but her legs had just stopped working. We had a lovely Christmas dinner. Ailsa and Mark had done us proud but at about 16:00 Helen announced that she wanted to go back to the hospital. We didn't know why as Helen was not one for ever needing to be home by a certain time or "before it gets dark" as many aged do, but for some reason she had had enough and so it was time to go. By the time both Helen and Mavis had been toileted and dressed it was nearly 17:00 and so we left the family and I drove back to the hospital, returning my charge about 18:30. The nurses were good to Helen and while they were undressing her ready for bed, they were asking her all about her day out. She seemed to have enjoyed herself so there was little further to do. I returned to the car. Mavis was sound asleep so the day had obviously taken its toll on her as well. Perhaps it was right to have left early after all.

There was nothing happening in the week between Christmas and New Year at the hospital for Mavis. What joy! Although the visits for Mavis to the hospital were so vitally important, it was lovely to enjoy just being in the house together apart from going to see Helen. The days had the impression of being long, and at times, a little drawn out. For the first time since Mavis had come out of hospital, it seemed we had the time to take things easy.

New Years Eve 2004.

For years now on New Year's Eve, we have had a get together with our friends. The group comprised of Bill and Pat our neighbours, Barbara and Alan from Sunderland, and Margaret and Keith from Bridlington. We took it in turns, going to each other's houses, apart from Margaret and Keith who, for expediency sake, always came and stopped with us. Fortunately or unfortunately, this year it was our turn and whilst I was prepared to do all of it, everyone insisted on doing their part. One couple brought the starter, another the sweet, another the drinks and I supplied the rest. It was fabulous to see Mavis sitting in state at the head of the table being able to converse, albeit very slowly, with all the company. I wondered how she would manage until midnight but she did very well. After they had gone home and Margaret and Keith had helped me clear up; as I prepared Mavis for bed we thanked God just how blessed we both were. We not only have such wonderful friends but God had spared Mavis to enjoy them for at least a little longer.

1st January 2005.

A new day of a new year and after breakfast, we all decided it would be nice to get some fresh air. There is a new park, about a mile from home, which has been reclaimed from an old open cast mine. We all got dressed and Mavis attended in her wheelchair as the rest of us walked. It was a nice clear day with some sunshine but cold, as you would expect for January. To cross the main road to the park we had to go along on the road, causing a nuisance to the traffic because there was no suitable ramp to allow the wheelchair onto a path. We started to walk around the park, which takes about an hour. Now whether it was the medication i.e. the Warfarin that Mavis is on or whether it was just sitting still in a wheelchair all the time I don't know, but when I looked around, Mavis had tears rolling down her face and an enquiry responded that she was extremely cold. We had no alternative but to return home as soon as we could. Since this had been the first real test of an Electric wheelchair from home to the park and return, it was disconcerting to note how difficult it was. On the way back, we took a less exposed route so that Mavis was more sheltered from the wind. It did mean going along several roads in a housing estate and it was appalling how many motorists had parked on the pavement so that you could not get the wheelchair through. In most cases this was not too much of a problem as Mavis could go down one ramp onto the road, along on the road and then back up another ramp later on. However, at one juncture where we had gone for quite a long way down the pavement, we were to be confronted with a car on the pavement and no way of negotiating around it.

Keith is a big man and so volunteered to knock on the door and ask the occupants to move their car. At about noon on New Year's Day I was wondering what reception we would receive but they were up and didn't seem to mind too much. As we got nearly home Bill and Pat spotted us and we were invited in for mince pies and ginger wine, which I think helped Mavis warm up a little. This simple walk had shown us two things. 1) No matter how many clothes you think you need, when you are sitting in a wheelchair, you obviously need many more and 2) to be far more careful ourselves where we park the car in future so as not to block wheelchair access.

Thursday 6th January 2005.

Our first appointment, back at the hospital after the New Year, this time it is to see the speech therapist. The speech therapy department is quite some way from the main entrance. As Mavis had done little exercise over the last two weeks and we had plenty of time to spare, I suggested that rather than take the wheelchair she could at least try to walk the distance. She was very reluctant at first but I comforted her by saying that the hospital was the best place to try it on two counts a) should she collapse there would be plenty of professionals around that could help her and b) if it just became too much I could go and fetch the wheelchair for her. She eventually agreed to give it a go. So off we went and she managed remarkably well and we were able to reach the department

127

reasonably on time. I think after the last visit our usual speech therapist had had enough of me and instead of seeing her, we were invited into the office of the chief gaffer. She said that she wanted to evaluate Mavis for herself, so the tests went on and on for nearly an hour and a half. At the end of the tests, she informed us that in her opinion, her department could not help Mavis any further. Mavis had recovered most of her brainpower and that the weakness was not in her knowledge but in the ability to communicate it.

I actually think this was a conclusion that Mavis and I probably already knew. She couldn't say whether this would improve any more or not but basically the more Mavis tried to talk to different people the more it was likely to improve. We left the department with very mixed emotions. On one hand, we were told that Mavis could not be helped any further and yet, on the other, there was still hope that things would continue to improve over time. As we were at the hospital already, we departed from our usual afternoon visits to Helen and went to see her straight away. Helen's ward was at the far end of the hospital from where we were. Mavis had walked quite some way to reach the speech therapy department so it followed that after having sufficient rest whilst doing all the tests, she should try to walk to the ward. It took us 45 minutes but we did make it. We passed the toffee nosed female consultant that Mavis had when she was on the first stroke ward but she didn't acknowledge us and we definitely didn't try to attract her attention.

Helen was sitting up in a chair and looking quite perky. No sooner had we started the visit than the ward sister came to see us and said that the "team" had decided that Helen was now able to leave the ward. They would not be sending her home but instead it had been agreed that she should go to a residential home instead and we needed to start making arrangements. I didn't know whether to fight the decision or not. Most of me wanted her home so that she could be looked after properly. The other part knew that especially if she displayed the tendencies she had shown over Christmas, I would not be able to manage both her and Mavis properly. Mavis had to come first. They said that Helen would be moved to a "half way house" early next week but she would only be allowed to stay there for two weeks. We would have to find a home for her fairly quickly.

We returned home and discussed the situation the best we could through the tears and heartache. Mavis was very despondent that she could not look after Helen herself. For me it was the fact that it was really both impractical and probably a little irresponsible to try to look after them both. So, in many ways the pain and guilt that so many families have to go through determining when to put a parent into a home had been taken away from us through circumstance. It perhaps didn't make the overall experience any easier but the point at which something had to be done had been made for us.

Saturday 8th January 2005.

Yesterday had been spent on the telephone most of the day making appointments for us to visit today. The objective was to go and see as many residential homes as possible from a short list we had been able to prepare earlier. This was from our previous experience of doing domiciliary eye care during a previous business venture, but you can obtain lists from the council. It was surprising how many people thought we were applying for Mavis because she was in the wheelchair, even though I had told them differently during the telephone call. Some of the homes were dreadful, others just bad, and a very few passable. We came back home very despondent but firmly resolved that Helen was going to live out the rest of her life in a decent atmosphere. It also brought home to us exactly how close it was that Mavis very nearly had to go into one of these places and how devastating that would have been for everyone, most of all her.

Sunday 9th January 2005.

More homes (if you can call them that) to see. One of which was where one of our elderly neighbours was placed about two years earlier after her husband had died, and she could no longer take care of herself. We warmed to this one almost immediately. It was in Washington about five miles from where we live and although there were homes closer, we considered it worth the extra distance to travel in order to try to give Helen the best. Unfortunately, all the best homes of course are full, so we put Helens name down on the waiting list and hoped, rather selfishly, that a vacancy would soon become available. This period allowing us to find Helen a home, rather than one being allocated to her by social services, was very short.

Monday 10th January 2005.

We were rung by the hospital social worker today to say that Helen would be moving to the half way house on Thursday and would we be available to move her. I thought it better if the hospital arranged transportation as if Helen decided her legs were not moving again, I would be stuck. They agreed to this and for Mavis, it was back to the physio. I was proud to announce to 'C' all that Mavis had accomplished over the Christmas break.

Thursday 13th January 2005.

Helen was moved and we went to see her in her new residence. She had her own room and her own en-suite which meant she didn't have far to go to the toilet. Useful as this is now proving to become an ever-increasing problem for her. She had her own telly and the staff seemed to be nice so, overall, we couldn't have wished for better. What was more important was that Helen liked it. It seemed as good a moment as any to break the news to her that she wouldn't ever be coming home again. She would instead, be going onto a residential home. We tried to console her with the fact that if everything worked out Ok, she would be living in a room that would be very similar to the room she was in now. She seemed to take it well but you know the shock of someone telling you that you will not be returning to your own home at the age of 85, must still take its toll.

Wednesday 19th January 2005.

My life seems to be taken up with visiting. If it is not the hospital with Mavis, it is going to see Helen. The time seems to fly. Today we had a telephone call from the home to say that they think a vacancy will be arriving in about a week, so good news for Helen.

Tuesday 7th February 2005.

We moved Helen from the "halfway home" to her new abode. The room had been freshly painted and is a single room with en-suite facilities so it's not too different from the room she had at home or the halfway house. We took all her pictures in, together with her own television and VCR and tried to make it look as much like her own room was when she left it. Mavis was very tearful; I suspect a mixture of pity and guilt, but on the surface seemed practical enough to be resigned to the situation.

I am slowly adapting myself to my new lifestyle although I realise that I still have many skills to learn. The most important seems to be that of planning. I know we need to eat every day but sometimes when it's time to eat, I realise that either I haven't been shopping or the food is still in the freezer. Thank goodness for microwaves. Mavis's physio sessions continue and she is still improving. She can now walk about 40 yards albeit in about 30 minutes but she is walking again, which is more than anyone ever expected. I don't think they will keep the appointments going for much longer as we seem to be taking up a tremendous amount of resources in an already terribly over stretched department. Life also seems to have settled down now a little with the visiting timetable. We see Helen every afternoon and the physio three days a week, usually in the mornings. 'V', the social worker has been tremendous. She has been keeping in touch with both Helen and ourselves. All in all life is about as good as I think it is ever likely to be, under the circumstances.

The daily routine is also relatively straightforward. Mavis wakes me up when she wants the toilet through the night. If it is somewhere close to normal rising time, we transfer from the toilet to the bath where Mavis sits on a bath board and I give her a shower. After the shower, it is drying and dressing. We then do the exercises ourselves if it is not a physio day. She lies on the bed and I try to move the left arm. It is very slow and very painful but Mavis tolerates it. We do these for about half an hour. If it is physio with an early appointment, then it is up at six thirty, leave the house about 9:15 for a 10:00 appointment. It is amazing how long it takes for both of us to be ready to go out.

Sunday 20th February 2005.

I have decided that now Helen has settled in well at the home it should be OK to take her out to church on Sundays, without her feeling too home sick. We talked it over with the staff during the week and they said she could probably manage it. This morning we were up early, went through the routine, and then drove to pick Helen up. When we arrived Helen was all ready looking clean and bathed. I loaded the second wheelchair into the car and set off for church. It was whilst driving there mulling on things through my mind that I realised there was little point having two wheelchairs, as I can only push one at a time. Mavis can transfer from a wheelchair to a "proper" seat so all the effort of lifting two wheelchairs in and out of the car seemed a bit pointless. Still you learn these things as you go on. Experience is a great teacher. When the service was over and everyone had made a great fuss of Helen, we took her back to the home. It was very tempting to bring her home with us but it wasn't possible. 1) we didn't have a downstairs toilet and I wasn't sure I could manage her from the top of her chair lift to her toilet upstairs and 2) there was still a very high risk of upsetting her due to the fact that she wasn't going to be coming home any more. We played on the premise that she was going back to her home and when we arrived, she was ushered into the dining room where we left her tucking into a vast plateful of roast beef and Yorkshire pudding. This was her favourite so all in all a good outcome.

Thursday 24th February 2005.

The rep for our business had made an appointment in Manchester and the nature of it was such that I had to be there as well. This meant having to take Mavis with me and so the haul began. Up at 5:00 and find appropriate clothing for Mavis to wear. Just because she is disabled does not stop her looking smart and we left the house at 07:30. It was still very dark, cold, and miserable but I managed to load the wheelchair into the car without freezing to death and the journey began. It seemed from experience that in general, Mavis needed the toilet about every 1½ to 2 hours, so the journey was planned around motorway services and it all went well, arriving at the clients work place for 11:00. We managed Ok moving the wheelchair into the premises and we all attended the meeting. Mavis stayed awake and to her horror, I asked her to write some things down as we went along. I made notes too which was just as well because when we came to read Mavis's notes back it was very apparent that her brain still could not cope with more than one activity at once. Listening and writing are still not compatible. Overall, though she did really well but at the end she was looking totally exhausted.

About 14:30, we wrapped up the meeting loading the wheelchair and Mavis back into the car. We arrived home just on six o'clock. I couldn't be bothered to cook so it was fish and chips on the way in. Despite sleeping all the way home in the car apart from the toilet breaks, as soon as the supper was devoured Mavis wanted to go to bed. She was absolutely exhausted but it was another landmark for her in that she had met other people outside her own little world. She had to interface with them, which although exhausting for her I could only assume would have been good for her.

Sunday 27th February 2005.

We had a telephone call from Polly saying that Ed her husband was about to book a holiday in Matlock for themselves, Wendy and John. Would we like to join them. Mavis and I discussed it; we then rang them back to say yes we would try it. This would be something to look forward to and another experience for Mavis.

Monday 28th February 2005.

The architect arrived today to see if there was a better way of extending the house and to show us his first draft plans. He had come up with some really good ideas and at last we seem as if we might be making progress. The project manager 'P' also came with him. This enabled everyone to have a good discussion about the project. We eventually settled on a plan that seemed acceptable. These ideas would now go for planning permission and out to tender for the builders. I hoped that it would not take too long.

Monday 7th March 2005.

I went out shopping and when I returned, Mavis was on the floor at the bottom of the stairs and in some discomfort, if not pain. I now had to work out how to get her up again. I managed to turn her round so that her feet were away from the stairs and after a rest lifted her so that her bum went onto the first step. Then after another rest I lifted her again onto the next stair and then again onto the top one. From there with her legs now straight and with the help of the banister rail, we could now both struggle to get Mavis upright. Once Mavis was back into her wheelchair, I asked how she managed to fall and why at the bottom of the stairs.

Now I have to go to China next week for the company and Heather is coming to look after Mavis. It seemed this had been playing on her mind and while I was out Mavis decided to show Heather how well she was doing and she would try to climb the three steps to the stair lift by herself. It seemed she had reached the second stair, her leg had given way, and she had lost her balance and fallen back to the bottom. Fortunately, she landed on her bottom, so apart from extensive bruising to the base of her spine, she had survived the fall comparatively unscathed but she would definitely feel uncomfortable for some time.

Saturday 12th March 2005.

I flew to China. Heather and Mavis took me to the airport. As I flew out it was one of very mixed emotions. In some ways, it was a relief from the responsibility of looking after Mavis and yet in reality, I really didn't want to leave her. It was only for 5 days but even so, I now realised how Ailsa felt going to Barcelona.

Friday 18th March 2005.

I returned and everything seemed to be OK apart from the floods of tears (from Mavis, not Heather) so obviously she was pleased to see me. Mavis's bum was still very sore but perhaps this was nature's way of reminding Mavis not to try such antics on her own again. Still you can't knock a Trier.

Monday March 21st 2005.

We are on our way to meet Polly, Ed and the others at Matlock Baths. Polly had also contacted Margaret and Keith our friends from Bridlington but, unfortunately, they could not make it for the full period. However, they have agreed to come and spend the day with us tomorrow. It was going to be quite a party. I have always done my own packing whenever I have gone away like last week, and now I have very great sympathy with those who have to pack for someone else. Tablets, knickers, nightdress, something warm, soaps, perfume. Still, packed we were and we were going to enjoy it. Just on 16:00 we arrived at the hotel. Polly, Ed, Wendy, and John were already there. We parked in the disabled bay in the car park and Mavis managed to walk the few steps into the hotel. As we came in Polly and Ed came to meet us full of apologies as Ed had forgotten to book a disabled room. We looked at all the rooms that were available and managed to find one where Mavis could use the toilet by herself. It was up two flights of stairs and I was very surprised when reception said there was not a lift. It took Mavis a long time to walk up and down the stairs but she managed it as they say, with a little help from her friends.

Tuesday 22nd March 2005.

Margaret and Keith arrived just after breakfast bringing the heavy rain with them. We went exploring anyway in the hope it would stop at some time. However, it didn't so we missed seeing the beautiful countryside and came back to the hotel early to huddle around a big fire and catch up on everyone's news. With Heather our daughter and her family living fairly close, we had invited them to join us so, in the evening, 13 of us sat down for the evening meal. With all the activity and noise Mavis slept well that night.

Wednesday 23rd March 2005.

The weather was a little brighter today, but as we were all going home, we decided to spend the morning looking around the abundance of Mills and factory outlets in the area. I had been looking for some lightweight trousers for Mavis for the summer for some time. All her existing trousers had a zip and fasteners that are impossible to fasten when you only have the use of one arm/hand. We managed to find three pairs that were in a sale at £5.00 each so we bought all three, as they were exactly what we were looking for and after lunch bid farewell to the others. We were supposed to have gone home, but we were also invited to Margaret and Keith's for the Easter holiday. We discussed it and decided that rather than go all the way north, just to come south again, we would head for Bridlington straight away, arriving early evening.

Thursday 24th March 2005.

When we awoke, it was obvious that the week had taken its toll on Mavis as she looked very tired and drawn. She cried frequently too during the day, but nobody knew why, although we appreciated it was symptomatic of her stroke and tiredness. I just hadn't realised how much the week had taken out of her, but it had obviously been considerable.

Monday 27th March 2005.

After doing things over Easter, it was now obvious that Mavis had had enough and just wasn't coping. Nearly every time you spoke to her, she cried. She seemed so brain dead that asking even simple questions were being met with a blank response, so we decided we would go home early. As it happened, it was just as well. It had been very windy at home and the drainpipe had parted company from the guttering, so it gave me something to do in the afternoon while Mavis slept.

Thursday 14th April 2005.

We had a letter from the council saying that the plans for the extension have been passed and so work can now begin. This is good and something to look forward to as Mavis is still using the commode in the cupboard under the stairs for a toilet. This is Ok if we are by ourselves, but is a bit embarrassing when we have company as everyone has to be ushered out of the room into the kitchen whilst Mavis "uses the facilities"

Friday 15th April 2005.

Another letter arrived from the council. This time from 'P' confirming that he had put the work out to tender with the deadline for the end of the month. Hopefully we should be contacted by three different builders. We live in hope.

Tuesday 19th April.

A telephone call confirmed that a builder is interested and he arrived later with his digital camera to take photos. Seemed a nice chap but we don't hear from anyone else.

Monday May 2nd 2005.

I gave 'P' a ring to find out what was happening. It seemed that the guy who came round had submitted a quotation together with one other. Kevin the guy with the camera seemed to be the better quotation and I agreed with 'P' he should get the job, as at least he was interested. 'P' agreed and awarded Kevin the contract. We now have to see how long it is before they can make a start.

Tuesday May 17th 2005.

A telephone call from Kevin said that they might be able to start next week. So nearly six months after Mavis had come out of hospital things looked at least as if we were getting somewhere and Mavis perked up a little in anticipation.

Sunday May 22nd 2005.

Quite unusually for Mavis, this morning during the service, she had the urgency to go to the toilet. She told me this but I think she was quite shocked when I told her she was old enough now to go by herself. She struggled to her feet and very tentatively took the first faltering steps on her own. I remained in my seat forcing myself not to look or to be concerned but waiting in dread for the potential fall. I heard the door at the back click and knew that Mavis has made it so far. Then, just behind me, I heard another chair move and looked to see Margaret from Cameo arising to 'shadow' Mavis. I had very mixed emotions. It was wonderful to think that someone else cared enough about Mavis to ensure that nothing happened to her, but horrified that they thought I didn't care enough to go with her. It reminded me of the first time you take the stabilisers of the child's bike. You hope and pray that they can ride it on their own, but you have to be prepared for the consequences if they fall off. After what seemed an eternity I heard the door click again and very slowly heard the tap of Mavis's NHS stick as she slowly returned to her seat. This was only a little achievement, but a great stride towards Mavis becoming independent again. If she could do anything for herself, no matter how small or difficult, then I and other people had to let her.

Monday 23rd May 2005.

Having waited in anticipation all day, the builders did not arrive so we went to bed despondent

Tuesday 24th May 2005.

I rang the builders at about 11:00 as no one had turned up yet to be told that they won't be coming this week as they are running a little bit behind on the last job due to the wet weather. Hopefully but no guarantees, next Monday

Monday 30th May 2005.

I rose early. It was a nice day and so I took the opportunity of having my cup of coffee for breakfast outside. 08:30 passed and no sign of the builders so I concluded that, yet again, they were not going to arrive. At 09:20; I got a telephone call to say they are going to turn up, and they will be here in about ½ an hour. I was not sure exactly what I expected but it certainly didn't meet it, when a small van and two chaps arrived at nearly 11 o'clock. They were the "advance party", and they had come to start digging the garden and removing the trees, bushes, and plant boxes from the front of the house, in readiness for when the main party arrived later in the week. We watched in sadness as the fir trees that had been planted so long ago to help protect the house from the ravages of the North wind as it screamed at the house during the winter months trying to divest it from its heat, slowly were cut down and formed this very high mound in the garden.

Tuesday 31st May 2005.

At about 07:40 a very large low loader arrived with a mechanical digger on it. It seemed it was for us so I signed for it, and it waited in the front garden for the work force to appear.

The Physical side.

I have to be honest, I have only been asked this question once but I am sure many others would have liked to have asked about it, had they found the nerve. It is like asking a woman arctic explorer how she spends a penny without getting her bits frozen. We would all like to know the answer but don't ask. So what can I tell you? Full intercourse was not on the agenda either inside the hospital or when Mavis came home. The paralysis had made even the simplest act almost impossible. (let alone any in the Kama Sutra) It has been difficult at times when you have to look at a body from two completely different perspectives, the first as a husband who still loves his wife and all the intimate parts of her body, and the second as a carer who has to wash, clean and powder all those bits without getting sexually involved. When I worked away from home lying in a hotel bed I was always wishing I was at home making mad passionate love to my wife. In truth often when I was at home I would be wondering why I was so tired and not making mad passionate love. It is something that you need to discuss in depth and in full honesty with your partner. I am sure there are sexual counselling programs for the disabled but because we have been able to discuss it openly, and sex before the stroke although very important, was still only a small part of our marriage, we have sorted ourselves out. So remember, the next time your partner wants sex and you are too tired or you have a headache it might be their last request or the last time you can fulfil it.

Chapter 10

The building work begins.

The work started in earnest, and it seemed to take up every waking moment of every day for the next 10 weeks. I think it is worth departing from the usual date format and moving into weeks commenting on what was achieved weekly and any associated problems that we (I) encountered. As well as the building works proceeding, we were at the physio's three mornings of each week and going to see Helen most afternoons, so it was a hectic time.

Kevin the owner of the building firm was a likeable lad but extremely 'streetwise.' He had done many jobs for the council before, and he was very much aware that there are many things that crop up in a building project that cannot be reasonably foreseen. They still had to be done and even more importantly, they still had to be paid for. Therefore, the project began. I have sketched the plan of the existing and the proposed below to give an idea of the layout. I haven't put in doors or windows as I thought it would be fun if you wanted to put them where you thought they would go yourself.

In other words, I'm lazy.

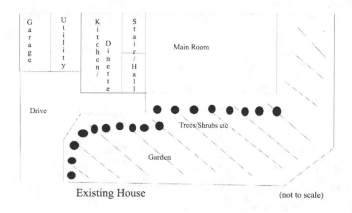

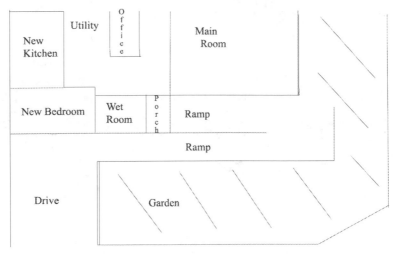

Proposed Layout

Week 1.

The builders arrived, removed the trees/shrubs from the garden, and turned the garden into a builder's yard. Problems - None.

Week 2.

The mechanical digger arrived, removed all the roots from the trees, and dug a deep trench for the proposed foundations. The existing drive block paving was lifted and stored for future use. A hole was made in the house walls between the utility room, the existing garage, the dinette and outside. The existing radiators were removed from the hall and dinette and the plumbing was capped accordingly. The digger fell over into a hole and therefore was out of commission for two days while we worked on ways to right it. Fortunately, nobody was hurt.

Week 3.

Mavis was very agitated as she was confined to the one room and the noise level high and incessant. Despite attempts from the builders to keep the dirt down, dust was now appearing at a tremendous rate and try as I might I could not seem to keep on top of it. As soon as I dusted yet another grey covering formed. The drainage pipes went in but we then found a problem. When the builder originally built the house, the water from the roof went into a very poor drain, which over the years, had become blocked, and must have been leaking under the soil in the garden, but we didn't know. Discussions now had to take place to decide who was going to pay for the old drain to be repaired, so that the new drain could be coupled to it.

Week 4.

The bricklaying started and the walls began to take shape. The rooms looked small, but they always do when it is simply the brickwork. I mourned the passing of the garage and wondered where I would now be able to store all the multitudinous array of junk that people usually keep in their garage. Discussing it with the builder, I came up with the idea of having a sort of cellar that could be accessed from the side of the house. We discussed this in depth and both agreed that it was possible, providing I paid for it. Therefore, the lads dug out to a reasonable depth under the floor, and then covered it with concrete. The floors joists put in and we began to see the eventual shape in real life, so to speak.

Week 5.

Consulting the plans, Kevin the builder asked what was happening to the back wall of the garage, as there was no provision for it. It was hard to believe but he was right. Everyone had missed it, so, if I wanted a rear wall to the new kitchen I would have to pay for it, another £800.00. The weather was awful. We were a delayed little, but not too far behind schedule. The dust was still mounting and I nearly gave up; but what can you do but keep fighting it. Fortunately, Mavis was still having physio three times a week, so we could escape from the house for a couple of hours on those days, and on the others, I tried to think of other things we could do and places to visit. It was a problem for the builders, as they had to keep an entrance free. It was impossible for Mavis to use the front door so we had to go out the back. I think she enjoyed being helped by all these young strong men.

Week 6.

The roof joists went on and the remaining brickwork was finished off. Windows and doors were ordered and it looked as if the end would eventually soon be in sight. The electricians came to start the wiring but found another problem. As our house was built originally in 1963, the wiring standards had changed since then and the lighting circuit was devoid of an earth. This meant that the new extension could not be connected to the old house until the house wiring had been updated. So again, who was going to pay for it? The old house still had a fuse board and it was evident that with only one hand Mavis would never be able to change a fuse on her own. We agreed that the house was to be upgraded and I would share the cost with the council. Another £400.00, but it needed to be done.

To help relieve the tedium of being in most of the time I took Mavis to look at new kitchens. I had measured the new room that used to be the garage and had spent the last week planning it all out. Not that it was of any consequence, as the kitchen people always wanted to show how good their software was, and everyone wanted to do the same thing over and over again. We emphasised repeatedly the necessity that ovens and hobs must be at a height that was convenient for a wheelchair user. Some noted this, and some did not, so you had to keep reminding them. We eventually settled on a MFI design and placed the order for delivery sometime in August, but until all the work was finished, we couldn't exactly say when. As was usual with MFI, they had one of their sales going on which included a cooker and hob. I had to do a great deal of research on the web to find out what exactly they were going to supply. One of the things they were willing to supply, providing we paid the difference, was an induction hob. This struck me as the best idea for Mavis, as there would not be any flames or hot surfaces to be burnt on and it would also switch itself off if it was not being used. It seemed ideal.

Week 7.

Whilst things like plumbing were going on inside, the main work of constructing the ramp was going on outside. Now it was always accepted that this was going to be a problem and really had to be left to the builder's experience, once the main construction had been completed. This was because the original house was built at the bottom of the hill. All the levels were difficult. To build the ramp, to the specifications, it had to be planned very accurately. By using the height of the drive to advantage, it enabled the ramp to look as if it was part of the house, rather than a ramble through the garden. After many calculations, it was decided which would be the best course, but this left another problem.

Where the ramp turned back on itself to come in to the front door, meant that the width would be nearly a metre wider. This therefore, meant extra paving and yes, someone had to pay for it. 'P' from the council and Kevin from the builders agreed it between them and so the ramp commenced. The drive and the gateway to the drive also had to be widened so that we could get the car on the drive and the wheelchair by the side of the car. Once it was all marked out the block paving started to be returned.

Week 8.

The windows and doors arrived and were fitted together with a new front door chosen by Mavis, which does look very nice (no expense spared!) The MDF floors were fitted over the joists and the wet room had its own special floor fitted. The special tiles arrived for the roof, (due to the very low roofline) and these also were fitted. Therefore, at long last, the house was once again resilient to the weather. I decided that as new radiators were going to have to be fitted in the new rooms and joined up to the existing heating system, it would be a good idea to drain the whole system and fit thermostatic valves to all the existing radiators. All the new ones would have them anyway. I hated draining our system as it is a single pipe system, and never refills easily without endless airlocks. It usually took about three attempts to have it working again afterwards. Bill came along and we worked all day removing all the radiators, cleaning them out and then replacing them to the walls with the new valves. True to form it took two days to service the system and another five attempts to have the system circulating again properly afterwards.

Week 9.

All the new walls and ceilings were plastered and the new shower connected in the wet room. The electricians returned to connect the lighting and sockets and to replace the old fuse board with a new distribution board. It had nice little circuit breakers that Mavis could now reset, should anything happen, if I was not at home with her for any reason. The tiling in the wet room was finished and the sink and toilet were fitted and plumbed in. Only one problem, the sink would fill OK but would not empty. All the pipe work was dismantled looking for blockages but nothing was found and everyone was completely mystified. Water should flow away downhill and for some reason, in this case, it had decided not to. 'P' from the council was summoned and even with his experience he was a bit mused as to the reason it did not work. A call to Keith in Bridlington availed the answer. It needed a "farting" trap. Now please don't ask me what a farting trap is as I could not tell you. Suffice to say I told Kevin who ordered one and it now worked a treat! As a bit of light relief for Mavis, her electric wheelchair from the council arrived and she was given an hour's instruction on how to use it. This was despite the fact that she had been driving her own for nearly a year now.

Week 10.

The ugly black railings that have to go up, by law, alongside the ramp were erected. The joiner fitted the skirting boards to the floors and made the doors fit properly. And so the builders departed, the house was once again ours together with about 6" of dust everywhere, and I mean everywhere.

Saturday 13th August 2005.

I rose early and with plenty of hot water, I started to wash everything down. It would be very interesting to know what would happen if a disabled person had to have this sort of work done and they lived on their own. There was no way Mavis could have cleaned the house on her own afterwards. About 10:30, the doorbell rang and it was Bill and Pat complete with dusters and rubber gloves coming to give me a hand and I was very thankful. Every conceivable surface had to be washed and then washed again. By 19:00, a very tired cleaning team collapsed with a take away. Mavis was very quiet that evening and just as we were going to bed I asked her why. Between floods of tears she blurted out that she a) hadn't been able to help and b) was so appreciative of everything that Bill, Pat, and others were doing for her. I listened attentively until I dropped off to sleep.

The next thing to do was to go and choose flooring to start making the new extension feel like part of the house. We decided on putting down a laminate floor as this would make moving the wheelchair much easier than going over carpets. Once I let on to Ailsa what we are doing she insisted that they would come over the next weekend to help me lay it.

Friday 19th August 2005.

I started the preparation and as soon as Ailsa arrived, we started work. As with all jobs you do, if you do it often enough you know what you are doing, but this was only the second time for me and the first for her, so we were learning as we went. We worked through until after midnight by which time we had the new room and kitchen about ¾ finished, but we were beginning to get the hang of it.

Saturday 20th August 2005.

We got up early and started straight away. By 15:00, all the boards had been cut and laid. There were only the skirting boards to cut and re-laid, so by 20:00 we had finished. Ailsa and I work well together until we get tired and we were both very tired. It was a good job we finished when we did but it was a good job done.

Wednesday 24th August 2005.

We stayed in awaiting the supply of the new kitchen from MFI and I must admit to being a little bit shocked, when it did arrive. The new kitchen was not very big but the boxes just kept arriving. By the time they had finished delivering, the new room was absolutely full of boxes, worktops, and kitchen appliances.

Acceptance not resignation

_Is our life different? Of course it is. Is it better? Probably
not. Is it worse? No. It is just different. We now lead
very different lives to those we lead over five years ago,
but my guess is that you probably do too. I realise that
the most difficult thing to do is to be content with your lot
but we have to try. From all the couples that we have met
through Dysphasia/stroke groups etc., the ones that seem
able to make the most of the life they have left are the ones
that seemed to have accepted their new life, rather than
those that have resigned themselves to it. I have seen those
that have been the most paralysed, still have the most sense
of fun, and those that seem to have the best and most of
everything material, often seem to be the most miserable. I
concede that I have been extremely fortunate in that Mavis
has been determined enough to try to make as full a recovery
as possible. So many will want to sit at home in front of
the telly and try to do nothing. My heart really goes out
to those carers that have to work hard 24 hours a day, 365
days in the year, with little or no support, for which the
government pays them £53.00/week at the time of writing.
Moreover, that's only until they are 60/65. Once they become
pensioners they lose all the carers allowance and have to do
everything they have been doing just on their pension. I
am not saying we have to be content with this, clearly not,
but being miserable either as a carer or the cared for doesn't
help anyone in the long run. When Mavis was just starting
to walk, the physios were walking her past this couple. The
lady had had a stroke some two years earlier but had made
a nearly full recovery. Her husband told me then that I
had to push Mavis not only physically but also mentally as
his wife never wanted to go outside the front door anymore
and you could see the despair in his face. Her stroke had
seriously curtailed not only her life, but his as well._

Chapter 11

Am I pleased we have such good friends!

It was going to be a painting weekend for the new rooms but I decided that the kitchen was a far better use of everyone's time and therefore this weekend was going to be a kitchen weekend instead.

Friday 26th August 2005.

Polly and Ed arrived from Leominster late in the evening so we were ready to start work early on Saturday morning.

Saturday 27th August 2005.

Bill and Pat arrived and we started unpacking boxes. Pat being the organised one, found the packing list and started putting the boxes together into groups until they resembled complete units rather than loads of little bits. Polly and Ed helped Pat unpack and assemble whilst Bill and I planned where they were all going and we put up batons to erect the units. By eleven we had three units up and then realised, they were not in the right place, so they had to come down again. 14:00, and Margaret and Keith arrived from Bridlington. Keith complained because we had not finished it before he arrived. We now started to motor. Polly and Margaret took Mavis to see Helen and the rest of us continued making up units and erecting them. By the evening, we had all the top units in properly (10) and the base units ready for fitting. Time to stop and party.

Sunday 28th August 2005.

Up early to serve breakfast for everyone. Ed said that Polly and he would like to go to our church this morning as they had heard so much about it but had never been there. They left, taking Margaret and Mavis with them, which left the rest of us to continue. We had a buffet lunch on the run and by around 16:00 we were ready to fit the workbenches and sink. I had bought a new router and a template for this very purpose and they all hovered in anticipation as I tried to get my first try in a straight line. Needless to say, the router bit jumped and ruined the template, so it was on to plan B. By 19:00, the sink was fitted and plumbed in and the two other workbenches were ready to be fitted. All being tired, it was down to the local Inn for some proper food and then Margaret and Keith left for home.

Monday 29th August 2005.

Polly and Ed were returning home today so after breakfast and another visit to see Helen they departed. We were left with a house full of silence. Mavis had coped well with the noise and bustle, but she was obviously very tired. I on the other hand had been uplifted that so many people were prepared to give up their time to help us. However, although the back had been broken there was still an amazing amount to do. All the electrics, including the cooker hood, had to be done and so I started work on my own. I have remarked before how much you miss your mate when you need another hand to hold something for you and unfortunately, this was something I was still trying to get used to.

We are now able to make use of the new downstairs facilities but to be honest, Mavis has improved so much over the last year, and I suppose we have developed such a routine that the urgency has now disappeared. The downstairs wet room and toilet are obviously an amazing help as it means that since Mavis is downstairs during the day she can now have a proper shower for the first time since leaving hospital. She can also go to a proper toilet instead of having to make use of the commode under the stairs during the day.

Tuesday 30th August 2005.

Bill arrived about 10:30 and together we managed to complete much of the electrics and cut the work top ready to fit the induction hob.

Wednesday 31st August 2005.

It is amazing that just when you think there isn't much left to do, you realise just how much there actually is. The devil is in the detail and sealing all the joints and making sure all the doors were aligned took another full day.

Saturday 3rd September 2005.

It was a nice day today so it was time to hire the cutter to cut a large hole through the wall for the cooker hood vent. Another job I had never done before. The special drill and cutter were as much as I could carry let alone use above my waist to cut the hole. Never mind we must persevere, otherwise the rest of the kitchen is going to start looking grubby very soon with all the steam and cooking smells unable to escape anywhere. After three hours, I managed it and returned the drill and bit to the tool hire company. Next time, if there ever is a next time, I will use a hammer and chisel. I am sure it would have been much quicker. Still the job looked the part and in the end, I was very pleased with it. The cooker hood was fitted (again, it would have been a lot easier if Mavis had been able to help but I _will_ get used to it... Eventually.)

Sunday 4th September 2005.

Helen wasn't too well so we didn't take her to church this morning but went on our own. After the service, Margaret, who runs the Cameo club at church, asked me if Mavis would like to attend. Quite honestly, I didn't know. Cameo is a club at church that meets every Tuesday. It is designed principally for the lonely and/or elderly. They are treated to various activities from leaning a new language to art classes and radio control cars. As well as super days out, they always get a slap up lunch before they come home every week. I could see that apart from the age thing, it could be good for Mavis as it would be someone new and different to talk with. If she could find something to interest her, it might help her brain to become better stimulated. I could see Mavis was terribly unsure, so we left it that Mavis and I would discuss it and let her know.

Monday 5th September 2005.

Helen is not at all well and the home has had to call the Doctor in. He thinks it is because of her blood sugars being all over the place and arranges for the Nurse to call every day to give her an insulin injection. This came as a very big shock as we were not even aware that she was Diabetic. We quizzed the home but could not find anything untoward, so assumed everything would be under control.

Thursday 8th September 2005.

We received a call from the home to say that Helen has had a fall and they have arranged for her to go to hospital to be checked over. When we reached the hospital, we found her in the geriatric ward not looking very well. It was too early for the staff to give us any diagnosis so we returned home and awaited further news.

Friday 9th September 2005.

We returned to the hospital to find Helen asleep and the staff all busy. We tried to find someone who could tell us something but if anyone did know, we never found them that day. On the way down from the ward to the exit, Mavis wanted to "spend a penny" and we had to go through the rigmarole of obtaining a key, this time from reception again. Why is it that only the disabled people seem to have to "walk the extra mile" as I noticed the ordinary toilets didn't have such limitations. I joined the queue at reception and eventually returned to Mavis with the key. By the time we were inside it was too late She sat there wet and heartbroken, crying her eyes out. Partly I felt from the indignity, but mostly from frustration and also I thought, it was the culmination of a very bad day. We got her dried out (electric hand dryers have never been so handy) (excuse the pun) and returned the key to reception. I asked the question why the toilet had to be kept locked but the receptionist didn't know, It was pointless shouting at her and so we went home full of gloom and despondency.

Saturday 10th September 2005.

We arrived at the hospital to find the main lifts were not working today. It is Ok for the able bodied as they can use the stairs. For us we have to find another lift and then try to find our way to the floor that Helen is on. We returned to our car and I left Mavis's wheelchair in the car and then "borrowed" one from the hospital. We then took the lift as far as it would go and left the wheelchair on that floor. Mavis and I then struggled up the stairs to the next floor and I then pulled the wheelchair up so that we could continue. Helen was not very well but perked up a little when she noticed us. Mavis was looking quite flushed after all the exercise and trauma of reaching the ward, and Helen remarked how well she was looking. By reversing the process we managed to find our way back down again and wondered when the lifts would be working again.

Monday 12th September 2005.

After long discussions about the house and the new amenities, we have decided to continue as we are for a little longer. Mavis only has to use the stairs once at night to go up to bed, and only once in the morning to come down again. We decided that we can manage as things are at present, believing that it will be good for Mavis if she attempts the stairs all the time. We have also agreed that the stair lift should come out totally to be stored for possible future use. At least the house will look a little less like a disabled one and that surely has to make Mavis feel much better. Not that there is anything wrong with a disabled house but by removing the disabled fitments as and when, it demonstrated progress on Mavis's behalf and marks another landmark in her recovery.

Tuesday 13th September 2005.

I asked Mavis is she wanted to go to Cameo club at church but she said No. We sat and discussed it at great length and while I could not find a definitive answer, it seemed she was really just scared of a) how she would manage and b) how other people would see her. I tried to point out that the others have seen her at church and that should anything happen they can always contact me if they needed to. We left it there for the moment.

Thursday 15th September 2005.

We received a call from the hospital to tell us that Helen has taken a turn for the worse and that we really ought to go and see her, so we attended as soon as we could. They hadn't over estimated. She looked so frail in her bed but what annoyed us was that she wasn't clean. We left the ward after about an hour and I remarked to the sister that I had expected Helen to be looked after and cleaned up when she became soiled. She sounded surprised it had happened, but said she would make sure in future.

Friday 16th September 2005.

What a difference a day makes. When we arrived at the hospital, Helen was sitting up in bed and looking in fine health. She said she felt fine and apart from being a little sleepy, she said she was looking forward to coming out and going back to the home.

The weekend was spent at the hospital, visiting, and so far Helen looks as if she will be coming out next week. It doesn't make any difference to us whether we visit her at the hospital or at the home, but it will be much nicer for Helen to be back in her own company and surroundings.

Monday 19th September 2005.

Helen was not too well again today so it doesn't look as if she will be coming out this week after all. On the way home I tentatively mentioned the Cameo club again to Mavis and to my surprise she said she would try it.

Tuesday 20th September 2005.

We arose early and I prepared Mavis for her first big adventure for some time, but in many ways this time she had to do it by herself. We had a few tears before we left and I began to think that she wouldn't go but, as she couldn't really tell me why she was crying, I helped her into the car and I drove her down to church and helped her out. At this point thinking everything was Ok, I returned home and started to do some housework. Strange, but the house seemed very large and quite empty suddenly. Keeping my eye on the time, I returned to church well before Cameo finishing time and tried to see if Mavis was enjoying herself. I could not see her anywhere. Eventually Mavis appeared with a red face and tears still streaming down her cheeks. It seemed that she had cried off and on for most of the morning. Mary, one of the helpers who is a fully qualified nurse and wonderful human being, had taken her into an adjacent room to try to stem the tears and find out what was inducing them. I am pleased in some ways to report that she had made no more progress than I usually could. Mavis cries. Sometimes Mavis cries for a reason and sometimes, although there may be a reason, nobody (probably including Mavis) knows what the reason is. I put Mavis into the car and thanked Mary for looking after her, then we headed home. Within two minutes of leaving church Mavis was sound asleep in the car, so it was not until later that I could start to find out how she had coped with the morning.

I woke Mavis and we had a quick cup of coffee in the house before going to visit Helen again. When we got to the hospital Helen was sound asleep in bed, so we didn't wake her. However, I noticed that the bed smelt and she was definitely not clean. We mentioned it to the staff again and they went in to clean her up so we left to come home, Mavis crying yet again. When we reached home and after Mavis has had a sleep, we discussed the day at length. Why had she been so tearful in the morning? Why had she been crying on the way home from the hospital? Crying on the way home, we got an answer for. It was because she felt guilty that she was not looking after Helen and that she felt Helen was not being looked after in hospital either. I tried to explain that even if Mavis had not had her stroke there was a very good chance that Helen would have been in hospital anyway because she had been so poorly. It was not her fault that Helen was not being kept clean in the hospital. The logic seemed to work and she accepted that providing we keep on top of it in the hospital things might improve.

Referring back to the morning, I can't really say we reached any conclusion. The tears seemed to be the manifestation of a collection of emotions. Going into a strange environment, me not being there, having to rely on others, they all seemed to contribute in some way, but she did agree to go next week, so a triumph in itself. 20:30 and Mavis was so tired she could not stay awake and wanted to go to bed. She slept until 11:20 the following morning.

Friday 23rd September 2005.

We received another call from the hospital. Helen has had another down turn during the night. She had not picked up during the early morning and the Doctor now thinks it could be very serious. We attended immediately only to find Helen missing and her bed empty. Mavis panicked and started crying while I tried to find a nurse. Yes, Helen was still alive; they had just moved her into a side ward. Mavis calmed down and after she stopped crying we went to find Helen. She was sitting up in bed but it was obvious she was not with it at all. Various questions were answered with unintelligent answers and we concluded that either Helen had had another small stroke or the medicine they are giving her was affecting her brain. I searched for a doctor who eventually took us to a small room and told us that Helen was not well because she now has C. Dif. He explained this was probably because of all the antibiotics they have been giving her over the last six months for the pneumonia and other ailments. These had probably killed off all the "good" germs in her body and therefore things were not good. We asked for a prognosis and he said they would continue to try to treat her but if she did not respond, then it was unlikely she would survive. Armed with this information, as soon as we were outside the hospital, I rang both Heather and Ailsa to inform them of their grandmother's possible imminent departure.

Saturday 24th September 2005.

Heather arrived about 12 noon bringing the grandchildren with her and Ailsa arrived a little later with both Henry and Mark. We all made our way to the hospital and when we arrived, Helen was sitting up in bed looking perky. She was so bright and with it that she appeared as if we have made a fool of everyone by bringing them all here under false pretences. When we went out, I assured them all that the Helen they saw was certainly not the same Helen we had seen yesterday and that the doctor had been really honest.

We all had an early meal and they all departed on their various ways as all were committed to church responsibilities the following day.

Sunday 25th September 2005.

After church we went to see Helen and she was fully cognisant knowing exactly what happened yesterday and that everyone had come to visit her. So perhaps she would get better after all.

Tuesday 27th September 2005.

As Mavis was still agreeing to go back to Cameo club, it was up early and I deposited her just before it was about to start. Mary assured me she would keep an eye on her for me and so I then returned home. It was too fraught staying in wondering how things were going on, so I went along to Bill and Pats for a morning of coffee and chat. So much so in fact that time marched on far quicker than I had anticipated, and after a hurried goodbye and quick dash to church, I arrived 10 minutes after they had finished expecting the worse. I walked into church to see Mavis sitting in a chair talking to a couple of others who all seemed to be enjoying themselves. What a complete transformation from last week. Mavis looked calm and confident in her surroundings. An aside talk with Mary, before Mavis spotted me, confirmed that although there had been some tears just shortly after I had left, Mavis had settled down and the rest of the morning had been fine.

Visits continued to the hospital to see Helen all week with very little change to report.

Monday October 3rd 2005.

Mavis's birthday today and cards arrived from everywhere. How fortunate we are to have so many friends and family that think about her.

Tuesday 4th October 2005.

I took Mavis to Cameo as usual and this time remembered to pick her up on time. There were not any tears at all this morning and she said she had enjoyed it. The Cameo club have several facilities for the clients to make use of and Mavis has decided she would like to join the Art class. She was always good at art. She was good at drawing and a long time ago now used to engrave glasses, and mirrors, to give as presents. For her to want to get back to 'art' could only be good for her. After visiting Helen who didn't seem quite as well as she had done at the weekend, we took ourselves off to the major 'art' store to invest in paints, brushes, paper and pencils. Now I don't mean to sound penny pinching but if you can go to B & Q and buy a 2", 1½", 2 x 1", and a ½" brush in a pack for under a fiver how come a tiny brush no bigger than a baby's little finger can cost upwards of £10.00? One I saw was £39.40 on special offer! Still it was Mavis's belated birthday present so I could not complain too much.

Wednesday 5th October 2005.

Helen was not well again today and we consulted with the doctor. He admitted that, although Helen had seemed to improve he hadn't really known why. However, he did now feel she had reached the point where she was not responding to treatment anymore. He suggested in fact, that the treatment should stop, as the C Diff was now taking over and there was nothing more they could do.

Thursday 6th October 2005

We went to see Helen and again have to contact the ward sister to say that Helen is in a filthy state. They put people in a side ward so that they can die in peace, but I often had thoughts that in Helen's case it was out of sight out of mind.

Friday 7th October 2005.

We went to visit Helen and today she is very weak. I asked her if she would like anything and she whispered she would like some chocolate. I checked with the doctor, as chocolate is not usually a good thing for very ill diabetics, but he said to go for it if she fancied it. It would not be the Diabetes that would kill her.

On Monday 10th October 2005.

Helen passed away. Mavis and I were at her bedside. She was in a deep sleep with her breathing very shallow. So shallow in fact that we were not sure of the exact moment she died. Mavis had been talking to her just in case she could hear her, and I do know that at one point she did say to Helen that there was no use in fighting any more. Mavis and I were fine and she was now managing ok. Whether Helen heard her we will never know but she departed peacefully to go to be with her beloved Jesus whom she had loved and worshiped all her life.

I will not bore you with the details, but sufficient to say that arranging the funeral, death certificates and everything else took up most if not all of the following week. Mavis was stoic in her approach to the whole episode but kept saying that still her only regret was that she was not able to look after Helen until her end. We had a new Pastor at the church so he had to be briefed and as Helen was Mavis's step mother, I had to contact all her old family in Scotland to try and obtain some appreciation of her life before she came to live in the North east with Mavis's father. The person who was actually going to conduct the service, Philip, was away in Dubai until the day before the funeral and therefore I had to make sure he had enough facts to go on for the service as well. Everyone I contacted was so helpful and it was difficult at times to try to reconcile the little frail old lady who died in the hospital bed with the vibrant, courageous person everyone could remember. Margaret and Keith arrived on the Monday to help me with the catering arrangements.

Tuesday October 18th 2005

The funeral was well attended. Heather sang a solo, as did Ailsa and then all the grandchildren sang at the end to cheer everyone up. We took them in the 'big car' with us as for most of them it was their first funeral and we wanted them to feel that we were celebrating the life of Helen, rather than mourning it. Again, God had been very good to us in as much as Helen had been taken out of the house some 10 months earlier. In many ways that had been the time to mourn and therefore there wasn't that terrible vacuum you feel when someone leaves. Mavis coped well apart from the usual tears we were still getting most days and life continued in the same vein we had got accustomed to, but without the visiting.

The rest of the year seemed to come and go. I had my 60th birthday and the children and their families laid on a super surprise weekend. I was sent with Keith to go driving cross-country in a Land Rover, while the girls looked after Mavis in a posh hotel in the Lake District for the afternoon. In the evening, we were treated to a wonderful meal in the church hall, for me and about 40 specially invited guests, summonsed to tell me how old I was getting. This was a wonderful occasion with all the family very much involved. Mark was 'head chef' with Heather and Ailsa helping in the kitchen. Mike (Heathers husband) was front of house Metre-de with all the grandchildren dressed very smartly as waiters, under him. There was a choice from the menu and everyone enjoyed a fabulous meal together. An embarrassing montage of my life, with very kind tributes followed this from a few selected speakers. Everyone stopped for the weekend and it was so enjoyable that I wished we could do it every time someone had a birthday. It had exhausted Mavis totally, but she was able to take part and I think that managing to 'keep the secret' improved her self-confidence no end.

Mavis and I slowly started to develop a different routine now, as there was no hospital visiting apart from Mavis's physiotherapy. We were conscious that even that wasn't going to last for long, because we could see that there wasn't a lot happening to justify its continuation.

In November, out of the blue, came a letter from a person called Margaret, telling us about a group called the Sunderland Speakability Group that is intended for people with Dysphasia. It met every 2nd and 4th Tuesday afternoon at a sheltered housing complex not too far from us, and we would be welcome to attend. This was different from the stroke club in as much as both Mavis and I were welcome. It seemed to be aimed at both the cared for and the carer. I again had to discuss it at great length with Mavis, but eventually she agreed to try it. It did mean a very rushed and busy Tuesday but if Mavis could cope it would give me contact with others of like predicament as well, and maybe I could compare how well or otherwise I was coping

December 15th 2005.

We went to the Speakability Christmas dinner today and although we had only met them all twice before, we were looking forward to it. I was feeling fine when we left the house, but by the time we arrived at the venue, I was feeling distinctly ill. I managed to endure the dinner, just, and then returned home as quickly as we could. Mavis was also now feeling unwell and probably for the first time in all our married life, we were going to be ill together. I now have some idea of what it must be like to be a single parent, be ill yet still have to get up, feed and look after the children. Fortunately, my illness did not last long and we were able to cope again relatively quickly.

Christmas arrived and all the family were coming to spend at least Christmas Day with us. I decided to do a traditional Christmas dinner and that meant forward planning. Everything came together well and all ten of us sat down on Christmas Day, rejoicing in the fact that Mavis had at least been spared and was well enough to enjoy Christmas in her own home with all her family. Opening all her presents with only the use of one hand did present problems but the grand children seemed very willing to help.

Mavis's input 1of 4.

It is now just over five years since I had my stroke and it is only in the last 6 weeks that Mike has allowed me to read his work, before he tries to get it into print. This has been both traumatic and moving. I have cried a lot. I think this is because it has brought home to me the realisation that it has not only been very hard for me, but for the rest of my family and friends. The stroke has made me very much more aware of how much I love Mike and the girls and life now has an immediacy to tell them, often. Life is still very fragile and we need to try to make the best of it every day. I remember particularly when it was my 60th birthday telling all our friends and family that they were the extra blessings God had given to me, but it wasn't until after I had my stroke that I realised just how precious those blessing are. God often brought into my mind these blessings when I had my "self-pity parties", so instead of dwelling on myself I would be distracted to the love of my family and friends.

The first few weeks in hospital, I can remember very little, but I do remember people whom I did not know but were obviously the chaplains coming to see me and inviting me down to the services. I also remember when Mike returned from his visit on his own to Margaret's Birthday party in Bridlington. He brought in a CD together with a portable player so that I could listen to it. The one particular track he wanted me to listen to was "He lifts me up" (before Take That made it famous). As I listened to it, he left the ward and it then became synonymous with him leaving me alone in what seemed a hostile environment. Even today, I find it extremely difficult to listen to without crying.

Chapter 12

2006...and a new beginning?

The major trauma was it seemed, now well behind us and we have to learn to focus more on what could be improved upon and what we now had to take for granted. Mavis and I continued to work on exercising her arm, as physio had now stopped with the statement that it was unlikely to start again as there was no improvement. We decided that the challenge this year was going to see if it was at all possible for Mavis to be allowed to drive again. It would also be nice to go abroad for a holiday again. With these two objectives in mind, the year started positively.

In February, I contacted the driving centre for the disabled in Newcastle and we fixed a date for an assessment that was going to be about 6 weeks later.

Mavis was now beginning to develop a little more stamina in her walking and so, on one nice day in March, I suggested she try and walk to the post box at the end of our road to post a letter. To my utter surprise, she agreed and so started probably one of her biggest challenges to date. She left the house at 11:40 with the letter stuck firmly into her coat pocket, and I watched from the window as very slowly, step-by-step, she left the house. I was very nervous about what might happen. Not wanting her to feel that I was spying on her, I also left the house but took a very different route. I watched her gradually getting closer to the end of the road. The beauty of the estate we live on is that all the front gardens have small walls, so that as Mavis became tired, she could sit on the wall and rest. And so it was, twenty paces and then a rest, another thirty paces and another rest. It was torture watching her as she tried to accomplish this simple task that you and I would take for granted. Usually it would take me about eight minutes and yet here some forty-five minutes later

Mavis was just approaching the post box. She had successfully negotiated the crossing of quite a busy road and I hid behind a house some distance away and watched with a tremendous sense of pride as Mavis deposited the letter. I can't remember who it was addressed to, but I do know the recipient had absolutely no idea of the amount of tenacity, effort and will power that had gone into the first leg of that letters journey. I returned home without being seen and awaited the triumphant return. After fifty-five minutes Mavis still hadn't returned and I was beginning to get concerned. Looking down the road I could see Mavis sitting on a wall not far from Bill and Pats, so I walked down to meet her. She was sitting there crying her eyes out but again I had no idea exactly why, although I had my suspicions. Once I calmed her down it became obvious that the tears were a mixture of jubilation at the sense of achievement and overwhelming exhaustion. I eased her off the wall and helped her take the next few steps to start towards home. Bill noticed us and came to see if there was a problem but when I explained Mavis's achievement we were ushered into their house for a celebration of coffee and cakes.

June came and the date arrived for Mavis's first driving assessment. Each time we had been out, either in the wheelchair or walking, we had practised her reading car number plates at a distance of about 25 yards. It was not that Mavis could not see the letters, but her dysphasia often meant that the wrong letters were said and if possible, this had to be avoided on the day. We arrived at the allotted time and I was not sure what I expected but what happened was certainly not it. We were ushered into a room where Mavis was given various tests, many of them so difficult I think I would have had problems. Grouping shapes and colours was easy but having to read a page of text from a book and remember at the end of it how many times you had read a particular word was something else. Mavis passed with flying colours and they were pleased to note that Mavis's left side deficit was now nonexistent. These tests then lead to other tests after which, at last, Mavis was put into a car and taken around the car park in an attempt to assess her suitability. I sat and prayed and after what seemed an eternity Mavis returned with her assessor and we went into a room with all the other people that had been involved in the testing and awaited the outcome. They were very pleased to report that on their initial findings they thought that Mavis should be able to regain her licence but the final decision would be made only after they had given her a more thorough driving test. This would take place after she had had some driving instruction from a driving school specialising in cars adapted for the disabled. They gave us a list of such instructors and we left elated that another possible landmark was achievable on the road to recovery. As it happened, one such instructor lived at the top of our estate, so we called in on the way home and arranged for Mavis to become his pupil over the summer months.

In July, Ailsa had to go again to Barcelona and thought it would be good for us if we went with her, as any problems associated with travelling with a disabled person would be better sorted with more than just me available.

We left very early on the Friday morning and arrived at John Lennon Airport in Liverpool to take the flight to Barcelona. The first thing we found was that you can't carry or pull a case while you are pushing a wheelchair. Fortunately, I had only packed the one case between us envisaging such a problem. We tried various ways of solving it. It was too heavy to sit on Mavis's lap with comfort so the solution we found was that Mavis would push the case and I would push her in the wheelchair. Effectively I was pushing both but hey, it worked. We arrived at check out to be told that because we were taking the wheelchair we would be leaving from a different flight departure gate and to go there and wait until we were contacted. The flight left at 07:00 and we needed to be at the gate for 06:00. As we had plenty of time, we had breakfast and arrived at our gate just before our allotted time. We waited and watched various planes arrive and depart. The time just seemed to fly past but at 06:45, I was beginning to become very concerned. I was certain that our plane was now being loaded with passengers and there was no one talking to us! At 6:55, all the passengers had been loaded and we watched in awe as the main staircase to the plane was removed. They had forgotten us!

As we watched, staff started to come to our departure gate and we relayed our concerns to them. One lady then opened the departure gate door and ran across the tarmac to our plane waving frantically to try to attract attention. After a very short conversation we noted the steps going back towards the plane and before very long we were being escorted across the tarmac ready for boarding. We had said that Mavis could climb the stairs to the plane, given time, and so started the arduous task of Mavis climbing the steps very slowly while all the rest of plane looked on. I am sure they blamed us for the delay and therefore late departure.

This was our first flight with a disabled person so we were not sure what to expect. I was very surprised at what treatment we did receive. It seems that different carriers have different regulations concerning where disabled people are allowed to sit, and for some reason this carrier did not want to make it easy. To be able to help lift a person from the seat the lifter should ideally be in front of that person so you would expect Mavis to have had a seat at the front near the door, where there was plenty of space in front. No! Disabled people were not allowed to sit there, "in case they blocked the exit". Ok I had to accept that logic, but now Mavis was asked to move across a whole line of seats to sit by the window. "Why can't she sit on the end of the row?" I had asked, "Because in an emergency the people in the inside seats may not be able to get out" was the reply. Therefore, poor old Mavis had to try to manoeuvre herself across three seats to the inside. She could not slide across them, only having the use of one arm and a very weak left leg. The seats were not leather which made it even more difficult to manoeuvre, and so it took another five minutes for her to be settled before the plane could even attempt to leave. I could not help thinking it's bad enough being disabled without being told that you are expendable in an emergency as well.

An interesting exercise next, as Mavis wanted to go to the toilet. Fortunately, I was the only one that had to move to allow her out but the whole trauma of edging along a seat to the aisle had to be repeated. When she reached the end, I helped lift her to her feet and we started the perilous walk to the toilets. We were told we had to use the ones at the back of the plane but since we were seated very close to the front, I ignored the instruction and we duly arrived. Now it is not easy using an airline toilet at the best of times, so I feared the worst. I opened the door, checked how easy it would be for Mavis, and noted that the sink was on her "good" side so it would help her for leverage to stand up again. I helped her in and closed the door behind her. After what seemed like an eternity the lock opened and Mavis with a smile all over her face returned to the aisle. Everything had gone well and she had enough strength to raise herself from the toilet, so her leg muscles must still be improving. We arrived in Barcelona and waited for the arrival of Mavis's chair. We were asked to wait until everyone else disembarked and then waited some more. Eventually a man arrived with a chair and we, together with two others, were lowered in the lift to where Mavis's chair was waiting. A simple transfer and we then progressed to the checkout. Another accomplishment!

The hotel was very posh and we were escorted to the "disabled" room. It was a lovely room, immense in every proportion. Everything looked fine until you opened the bathroom, and immediately noticed that the shower was the over the bath type, and the bath was half inset into the floor. I could see the fear in Mavis's face already as getting in would be difficult but getting out of a wet bath would be even more difficult, as we had experienced before. I went to reception where they assured me that the room we were in was the only disabled room available and therefore we were forced to stay put. Mavis needed a shower before we could go out so we agreed that she would sit on the edge of the bath and I would shower her with the showerhead, hopefully, always pointing it in towards the bath, similar to the way we used to have to do it at home. There were plenty of towels so I put them all over the marble tile floor and we started. It was much like washing the car. I wetted Mavis all over, applied the soap, and then washed her all over. I then got the showerhead again and sprayed her all over. Lastly, I dried her off with the towel. I took Mavis back to the bedroom and got her dressed, returning to the bathroom to tidy up the mess. Fortunately the towels had absorbed most of the random water so after ringing out they were all hung to dry. Goodness knows what the chamber person thought on going into the room to find all eight towels absolutely ringing wet hanging in various places hoping they would quickly dry in the Spanish heat.

The rest of the weekend passed in a similar vein really. There were coaches laid on to take us to the various venues and Ailsa had to go to the evening show without us as she had established a) Mavis would not be able to manage the stairs, as they were too steep and b) there was no access for the wheelchair. Never mind, giving Mavis another car wash soon passed the time and the others, with Ailsa, were all soon back in the hotel and we were all taken for the evening meal. Very nice!

Mavis had a comfortable night and we amused ourselves while Ailsa worked all day on the Sunday. Apart from the showering episodes, everything else worked reasonably well. Soon it was Monday and ready for the return trip. I must admit the Spanish were much better organised. We were told where to wait and all those in wheelchairs were accompanied by a strong gentleman who pushed them all onto what resembled a large open pickup truck, via a tailgate. It was very similar to those wagons you see loading the food onto aeroplanes, and it worked the same way for loading us as well. All the wheelchairs were put into the loader and then raised to plane level and unloaded at the top. Once on the plane, we were ushered to the same position seats by the staff and told the same story. This seems to suggest it is company policy to make the journey as difficult for their disabled passengers as possible, presumably hoping that next time they will fly with someone else and they won't have to bother. As it happened this plane had leather seats and therefore Mavis could slide along to her allotted one more easily. Returning to the UK ecstatic is the only way we could describe it. We had taken on the challenge and apart from a few hiccups had triumphed, so we could do it again.

Back to the mundane for me but not for Mavis who was going to have her first driving lesson. John, the driving instructor, picked her up on time and off they went. I could feel the apprehension with Mavis as she sat in the car and I watched from the window, as he explained the use of the disabled controls. The next thing they were gone and I waited anxiously for their return. They both came back with smiles on their faces so it couldn't have been very bad. They explained they had just gone locally around the streets to allow time to become accustomed to the controls. John reckoned that Mavis probably needed another five lessons and if that were agreeable, he would book her in. Mavis was keen so the deed was done and we waited for the next lesson with great anticipation. She crawled into bed that night a very tired lady.

Next week John called for her, as planned, and off they went. Some one and a half hours later, they returned with John complementing Mavis on her accomplishment. It seemed they had been out on the main roads amongst the traffic and she had done really well. His considered opinion was that if Mavis continued to progress as she had, then there would be little doubt about her regaining her license.

The lessons continued and, as he had promised, after completing five John was confident that Mavis could now pass the test. We said goodbye to him and contacted the centre in Newcastle again. Eventually an appointment came through for September and on the day I drove

Mavis across, saw her transfer to the test car, and leave the car park. There then followed an interminable wait and, after what seemed days rather than hours, Mavis and her co-driver returned. We all went through into the same room as last time and sat awaiting the outcome. Mavis started to cry and again I couldn't tell if it was relief or frustration. One of the ladies asked Mavis why she was crying and between sobs she said she didn't think she had done very well. My heart sank for her. The examiner arrived and after the pleasantries were over, they told Mavis that she had passed the examination and they would be sending their report out in about 3 weeks. They would also send a copy to the DVLA at Swansea and that we should make application for Mavis to get her license back, which of course we did.

Mavis's input cont/

_It wasn't really until I was moved to the rehabilitation
unit in Monkwearmouth that things started to improve. I
was still very fearful when Mike wanted to take me out to
the restaurant for the first time, but I did appreciate that
it was probably best for me even though the trauma was
considerable. I was always encouraged by the staff in the
hospital, which made it very important. They made it so
exciting that the hurdles seemed so much less. They were
also very attentive to my ramblings when we returned, which
in some ways made the whole experience even more exciting._

_I can honestly say that I have been very much loved and
cosseted throughout the whole experience. People have been
prepared to wait until I finished my sentence instead of
trying to finish it for me. I can talk a lot faster in my brain
than through my mouth and God has always been there to
listen to, and understand me. There are many people who
have prayed for us and still continue to pray for us so my life
continues with small improvements happening all the time._

_One of the things I most wanted to do on leaving
hospital was to be able to stand in Church and
worship my God. Within a few months, he enabled
me to do this and, with the aid of my stick, I could
soon walk to the front to receive communion._

_I have been fortunate that Mike has always felt that
there is little that I cannot do but that everything
new is a challenge to be mastered. As such, our
life has changed. Not necessarily for the better
or for worse, but it is certainly different._

Chapter 13

Mavis joins the gym.

October 2006. The trouble with sitting around all day is that you are inclined to get fat, even eating very little. Mavis had always been inclined towards the curvy side so it was little surprising that the trend was upward. Her weight had been fairly stable since she came out of hospital but over the last three months she had suddenly put on nearly a stone and yet our eating habits had not changed at all. It was just as if her body had stopped using energy. On mentioning this to the doctor he suggested that if possible Mavis might like to join the gym. I could see the shock on her face when it was suggested but, to her credit, she agreed to try. We went down for a pre trial analysis and the instructor took her round all the various equipment. With a great deal of help on and off the machines it was evident that Mavis might see some benefit from this. So, with a little gentle persuasion, she agreed that it was worth a try.

On her first real day there, I was instructed on how to get Mavis on and off without damaging either her or the equipment; and so another journey began. We went three times a week and each time I wound up the machine a little more. It was useful that she still couldn't count because now, whereas when we first started going she was burning off just over 70 calories per session, after about a month she was burning 300.

All through October and November when we returned from the gym, we looked forward to seeing if the post had brought any news from the DVLA, but not even an acknowledgement. I tried to ring them but was told that it had nothing to do with me and that they could not answer to me on Mavis's behalf. I tried again a week later and a slightly more helpful operative who said Mavis's papers were with the medical division answered this time. Unfortunately that was as much as they were prepared to tell me. They would not even tell me how much longer they thought it was likely to take.

Wednesday 29th November 2006.

It was time to take action. I rang again but this time I insisted on obtaining the name of the head person to complain to. I wrote a long letter of complaint to him, on Mavis's behalf. It was a very good letter, even if I say it myself, and we laughed at the thought of the people in the DVLA thinking it could possibly have come from Mavis, but she had managed to sign it so it was good enough.

Wednesday December 13th 2006.

We had an acknowledgement saying the letter was being passed on to someone different from the person we had written to, as he had left. I was expecting another long delay.

Tuesday December 19th 2006.

We received a letter of apology from the new chap saying he would look into it.

Wednesday December 20th 2006.

We received another letter saying that Mavis can now drive again. It was a wonderful Christmas present for both of us!

I had done my research over the Internet to find out about what controls Mavis needed for the car and who could fit them. As soon as we had read the letter, we donned hats and coats and went to Gateshead to order the unit. I was hoping that they would be in stock so that Mavis stood a chance of driving over to Ailsa and Mark's on Christmas Day for lunch. It was not to be. The earliest we could make the booking for was January 4th 2007.

Mavis's Input cont./

Coming home for the first rime was a very big stepping-stone for me, and was quite eventful. I remember it well because Mike didn't tell me it might happen. He didn't even tell me we were going to go to the car and try the transfer. It was only when I was sitting in the car he asked me where I wanted to go and I said Home. I knew it was only for a short visit but it meant so much to me because it was proving to me that I could one day go home. I could not explain it to him then but it meant so much to me. It is a funny feeling when you are in hospital for a long time you feel as though people might have forgotten about you. You know they haven't but all the same, you have this very strange feeling. Everything seems just to revolve around the ward and home seems to become detached from you. Even your place within the home comes into doubt. Now that I am home, Mike still has to make decisions for me, as my brain does not yet seem capable of making them for myself. Even something as simple as sorting out Sunday lunch, that he made me responsible for, seems to evade me. I know I have to but I forget. Thankfully, Mike usually has a fall back so we don't go hungry.

The one thing I still find very hard to accept was having to put Helen in a home. She took me on when she married my Dad and it came full circle when we she lived with us just after my Dad died. She had been an integral part of the family and I didn't want her to go, but I knew we couldn't look after her. We visited her every other day and took her to church as often as we could. We tried to make this move for her as positive as we could, to try to make the last days of her life as colourful as possible. She had been a great encouragement to us so we felt her life should be as joyful as we could make it.

Chapter 14

A New Year a New Challenge.

Christmas and New Year passed normally and on January 4th, we picked the car up with all the new controls fitted. I tried to persuade Mavis to drive home but in fairness, it was dark and rush hour so I relented and drove home myself. I tried driving using the new controls, not easy at all and I wondered how Mavis was going to manage. I mentioned in a previous chapter about all the extras on the car that I didn't want but had been conned into buying. Well I have to report that it was not a con as such. God knew what we were going to need from the car in the future and in his wisdom had provided. The telephone that the garage had to fit now became an essential tool, in case Mavis ever had an accident or became lost, as she could still not remember how to use her mobile telephone. The memory seats that were not going to be of any use because I was going to be the only person driving, were now going to be made great use of. Mavis and I frequented different driving positions and by moving the seats, it helped enable Mavis's entry and exit to and from the car. In fact, the only extra that we didn't really need was the extra power in the radio, but if you remember, without that we wouldn't have had the telephone fitted, so all a means to an end.

Back to the Bank.

If Mavis was going to be able to go out driving herself before too long then it stood to reason that she needed some way of paying for petrol in the car, should she ever need to do so. She cannot remember numbers (even our telephone and postcode numbers still elude her) and so we had to think of something else, as nobody accepts cheques these days. Again, after a long search on the Internet, it seemed that some banks did have a credit card that uses chip and signature, rather than chip and pin.

We went over to the local Barclays branch and spent a long time talking to the girl. She assured us that Barclays did such a card and that she could apply for one for us. It seemed a good idea so we let her do the form filling and awaited the results with high expectation.

Saturday January 5th 2007.

It was a bright cold day as Mavis took to the road behind the wheel, very tentatively and very slowly. This was the first time I had accompanied her driving since her stroke. I must admit I was concerned, No, terrified! One problem we had already encountered was that Mavis could not fasten the safety belt herself. She had lost the ability to turn her trunk properly and therefore her right arm was not long enough to go around the body to click the belt. It was fine her being able to drive but only if someone was always there to fasten the seat belt for her. This made a mockery of gaining more of her independence. We made our way from the house and took the quiet roads down to the river where I had taken the children when I taught them to drive. I don't know what happened when she was being examined or when she was out with the driving instructor, but it soon became very clear that Mavis was going to have severe problems in reversing.

Mavis had been taught to turn round to reverse when she learnt to drive and therefore had always done it that way all her driving life. Now though, because she couldn't turn that far, she needed to reverse the way I had always done, just using the mirrors. The road I chose to practise this was narrow, very quiet and it ran alongside the river. Cars had been known to go off the road into the river over the years and so I thought this might help focus Mavis's attention more. The river was in high flood as we drove the quarter of a mile or so to a suitable juncture and stopped. All Mavis had to do was to reverse the car back to where we had come from. Three hours later, we had managed to do less than fifty yards in one attempt. This was going to be a major problem. I remembered thinking I was glad it was an automatic gearbox as I doubted if the clutch on a manual box would have stood the pressure. When we returned home she was totally exhausted and so, while she slept in the chair, I went on to the Internet again and tracked down a seat belt extension. They are supposed to be used to extend the length of the seat belt. However, by putting the buckle of the extension into the stationary part of the car belt I thought it would extend that part long enough for Mavis to be able to clip her belt to it. We would have to wait until it arrived to find out if it would work.

Sunday January 7th 2007.

We rose a little bit earlier as Mavis was going to drive to church this morning. Not bad for a beginner. It was very slow, barely 20 mph and the queue of traffic behind slowly became longer and longer, a little like following a hearse I suppose. I tried to ignore that and sat proudly in the seat watching Mavis driving again. After church Mavis drove home and parked outside the house. Again utterly exhausted, she slept all the afternoon but we both felt it had been worth every minute of her effort.

Monday 8th January 2007.

We went to the road down by the river again and to be honest Mavis's reversing was not much better than previously. It looked as if it would be a long haul before Mavis is able to reverse properly again. After a couple of hours the gearbox began to smell hot, so we stopped for the day and returned home to find that the seat belt extension part had arrived. I fitted it and Yes, Mavis is now able to fasten her own seat belt so from now on she will be able to go where she likes, when she likes. Another achievement.

Tuesday 9th January 2007.

Mavis had to take the plunge sometime so we agreed that today she would drive herself to Cameo club at church. I watched from the window as Mavis lifted herself into the car, fastened her seat belt and tentatively drove off the drive. She stopped a little way along the road and after some time I left the house to find out what was wrong. She had noticed that she hadn't taken the hand brake off so had stopped but try as she might she could not release it. This was probably my fault as I was the last person to drive it and I had probably pulled it on a bit too tight. We released the hand brake and Mavis trundled down the road. I watched as she negotiated around the parked cars and disappeared out of sight. I prayed for her safe return.

Cameo usually finished around 13:30 so I expected Mavis to be home about 13:50 as it is only ten minutes by car to church. 14:00 arrived and I was beginning to become very concerned. As I said, the car has a telephone in it that I could ring her on, but I didn't want to possibly distract her at a critical juncture. I bided my time and then slowly the car came down the road. I moved away from the window so she didn't know how worried I had been. The next thing I knew Mavis was in the house. The tears this time told me she was elated because she had done it.

Wednesday January 19th 2007.

The post arrived and we opened a letter from the bank saying, "here is your new credit card and your pin will arrive under separate cover". As it looked as if it was a standard letter I assumed it had just been an omission to say chip and signature instead of chip and pin. Mavis put it her purse as a new found treasure. She now at last felt she had a little of her own dignity and independence back.

Thursday January 20th 2007.

The letter with a pin number arrived so I called the call centre to check if a mistake had been made. Oh dear yes it had. They would send another card out straight away, as the one they have already sent was a chip and pin. No good for Mavis then.

Wednesday 26th January 2007.

Another card arrived this time with exactly the same letter as the previous card had, telling us that the pin number would be sent under separate cover.

Thursday 27th January 2007.

Yes, you've guessed it, the pin number arrived in the post. I contacted the call centre again. This time the person at the other end hadn't the foggiest idea what I was talking about. I lost my patience and asked to speak to the supervisor. No help here either but she would look into it and would ring me back.

Friday 28th January 2007.

I heard nothing.

Saturday 29th January 2007.

I rang the call centre again. This time my call was answered by someone who was willing to help but in the end concluded that there must be no such thing as a chip and signature card therefore I must be talking nonsense. This was the last straw and as soon as we were able, we stormed off to the local branch of Barclays Bank. I parked the car and transferred Mavis into the transfer chair (which is a lightweight one that I can push) and charged at great speed towards the bank. When we arrived I asked to see the manager and behold, managers do not work in Banks on Saturdays. This does diffuse the situation somewhat as I now have nobody to shout at or vent my anger on. As it happens, the girl who originally took all the details and applied for the card for Mavis does work on Saturdays and was on duty. She guided us into a corner with a desk and poured oil on my troubled waters. She checked and yes, she had applied for a chip and signature card and therefore could not understand why Mavis had been sent a chip and pin card...twice. I suggested it was probably because nobody else apart from her and me seemed to know that a chip and signature card existed. She said that she would sort it all out and would let me know.

Thursday 3rd February.

Mavis received her chip and signature card and she was now independent again.

Back to the driving.

Over the next month, we went out every day to practice reversing in particular, and driving in general. Mavis now seemed to be settling in and drives a little faster. Still relatively slowly, but better that than tearing all over the place having accidents. We discussed the slowness and came to the conclusion that although Mavis is able to see what is happening, her brain takes a little more time to assimilate it and therefore it means her driving slowly. She has also found that she can't drive with the radio on as this she feels causes a distraction that the brain cannot cope with yet. It's also the same with the Sat-Nav. Yes, Mavis can drive but needs every ounce of concentration to perform adequately.

Now that Mavis has a little more independence, we seriously considered whether she still needs the wheelchair. For small distances, she could use the mobility scooter and for the longer ones she can take the car. Not having to constantly load and unload the electric wheelchair into the car would certainly help my back. Yes, having the electric wheelchair did facilitate the longer journeys, but the days of the five-mile walks at weekends we conceded have ended. We reached the conclusion that the electric wheelchair is not really used enough and so I took a few photographs and sold it on E Bay. We only made half of what we paid for it but we knew it went to a "good" home.

February 2007.

Ailsa has a sort of time-share arrangement and she arranged for us, together with the "gang", to go to Lanzarote for a week. We were to fly from Manchester and take Mavis's mobility scooter. Everything went very well at Manchester and the staff were very helpful and friendly. The scooter had to go through the X ray machine, which was rather difficult, but manageable. The staff on the plane were great and could not have been more helpful. Mavis was given an aisle seat this time, which made things very much easier, and so we concluded that the "rules" governing disabled people in aircraft seem to be made up by each individual carrier rather than being proper aviation law. So far, so good. We were all on the plane and there was nothing that Mavis could not have accomplished on her own should she have wished to do so. However, when we reached Lanzarote it was a completely different story. Mavis disembarked from the aircraft after everyone else had left the plane as last time, but she was just left in the luggage hall. We all awaited our luggage and somehow expected Mavis's scooter to arrive either on or near the carousel. When the entire luggage had been claimed and the scooter was still nowhere to be found I started to worry. I tried asking several of the airport staff to no avail, but I was eventually directed to an office with a large queue forming at the window.

After nearly half an hour, the girl at the window told me that all such luggage as Mavis's scooter would be on carousel 6 and that was at the far end of the airport. I hurried to No 6 and looked in disbelief at the scooter. There it was right enough, but sitting on a conveyor belt that was about 3 feet off the ground. Even for me climbing up onto the conveyor was difficult enough. I then had to dismantle the scooter in order to make it light enough to lift down onto floor level. Mavis would never have managed that herself. Having reassembled the scooter again, I took it back to where everyone was waiting. We then proceeded with all our luggage to the car hire desk. Having completed the paperwork for the car hire and mounted the entire luggage we then tried to exit from the car park. It appears the car hire people put a parking ticket inside the car so that once you get to the exit barrier you can just leave. Unfortunately with the huge delay in retrieving the scooter, we had arrived at the barrier too late and the ticket had expired. More delay while I tried to explain to the lady in reception, in my best Spanish, that we couldn't get out of the car park. After many minutes, it was agreed by both of us that her English was far better than my Spanish, and so eventually, I was given another ticket and we were on our way.

The disabled accommodation we were booked into was absolutely superb. Everything was catered for, even a hydraulic lift for those unable to walk down into the pool so they could be lowered.

We did so much that week and it involved reasonably early starts for Mavis and late nights. She coped well, but as the week went on you could see she was struggling. It is always very difficult to try to organise a group of twelve people to do or go anywhere. I think by the end of the week Mavis could not have cared less where we were going, or who with, but she survived it all remarkably well. As we returned home to the UK, we returned the hire cars. We then went to the terminal to find that our plane was delayed by nearly seven hours. When we did start to move, the airport staff this time kept Mavis on the scooter, and she had to drive it onto the tailgate lift on the back of a lorry. This then lifted her onto the lorry itself and she was then transported to the plane. The whole of the tailgate then lifted her to plane level and Mavis arrived. The scooter was then packed into the hold and we took off for home. When we reached Manchester Airport, we were met by a gentleman with a wheelchair who pushed Mavis to the luggage carousel and while we were waiting for the luggage he disappeared, to come back some ten minutes later with Mavis's scooter. We had been scheduled to return to Manchester just before 18:00 hours. It was now past midnight and considering how late is was and how tiring the day had been, Mavis was still reasonably with it.

The 'day' was not however finished yet, as we had been invited to a very special birthday party, in Scotland, that had started on the

Thursday we were returning and would continue until the Saturday. We had calculated that if we had reached Manchester on time we would be home by about 20:30 on the Thursday evening. Then, after a quick change of suitcase, we could have been back on the road to arrive at the hotel in Scotland by around midnight. As it happened, we were now just leaving Manchester at 30 minutes past midnight and it was already Friday.

With there being little traffic on the road, we arrived to a very cold home just on 03:00. Mavis made a cup of coffee while I changed the suitcases and by 03:30, we were back on the road again. Mavis slept most of the way to Scotland and at 06:15 we arrived at the hotel. The first thing I noticed was that there were no disabled parking bays so I parked outside the door and Mavis and I went in. We booked in and when I mentioned about the disabled bays, or lack of them, I was told that this was because the hotel parked your car for you and therefore they were not necessary. Posh hotel this. We went to our room and as we had deliberately booked a disabled room what we found was a little disconcerting. The bed was extremely high and in the bathroom you would need a stepladder to reach anywhere near the bath. The shower of course was over the bath and the taps were the old-fashioned screw top taps that meant, for anyone with a weakness in their hands, they could not even get washed. I left Mavis sitting in a daze and returned to reception to explain the mistake that they had not given us a disabled room. "But we have" insisted the receptionist and when I asked her to justify how any part of the room was suitable for a disabled person, I was given the reply. "We have allowed extra room around the bottom of the bed so that a wheelchair can move around" I was too tired to argue and so returned to the room, helping Mavis to undress and lifting her into bed. We slept for two hours and then went down to breakfast. Our host greeted us somewhat surprised, as he had already checked to note our arrival time. On hearing of our disabled room problem, he summoned the banqueting manager and we then spent the next forty-five minutes explaining to her what a disabled room really meant. In the evening was the main entertainment in a large function room. As you exited the room, on the same floor level were both the ladies and gents toilets. Where were the disabled toilets? Up four steps and with no lift!

I have often wondered since what the true definition of a carer is and whether my antics with Mavis would qualify. In fact, I would think a good lawyer could win a case against me on the grounds of sleep deprivation alone. Apart from the disabled room nonsense, we had a super two days that finished off the whole holiday experience really well.

With all the extra food consumed over the weekend and the holiday, we returned to the gym in earnest. All was well until one day, after Mavis had been to the gym, she developed acute dizziness when changing from the vertical to the horizontal and vice versa. We monitored it closely, exactly when it happened and when it did not. It seemed to happen the day after Mavis had exercised, either at the gym or with me at home. I mentioned this to the doctor who then sent Mavis to the hospital for all sorts of hearing checks and they eventually agreed that the dizziness was due to debris inside the inner ear which, when it moves, often when people are exercising, makes people go dizzy. After a long consultation with the specialists it is concluded that Mavis should stop the exercising and see if the dizziness would disappear altogether. It did, and so half reluctantly Mavis stopped going to the gym and I revised our home physiotherapy regime.

April 2007.

Mavis received a letter from the DWP telling her she had to fill in the enclosed form to see if she could continue to receive her benefits. Here was where I made a very big mistake, as I felt that Mavis had progressed enough for her to try to fill the form in by herself. This she did and did it very well, or so I thought, and we posted it off without giving it any further consideration.

June 2007.

Life continued much as usual until the letter from the DWP arrived. This stated that as a result of their enquiries, Mavis was now deemed perfectly capable of doing everything for herself apart from being able to cut up her food. They said that if Mavis wanted to go out by herself she could do so, and that having me go with her was only a whim on her part and was not essential to her way of life. According to them, she could cook for herself, bath herself, dress herself, and basically do everything a fully able-bodied person could do, apart from cutting up her food. We sat horrified, read and re read the letter, and I wondered how anyone could make such a decision without even meeting the person concerned.

There was no medical, no consultation and we were both devastated. Mavis cried for what seemed like weeks saying she was a drag on both society and myself, and that it was all her fault. Trying to keep her morale up was a full time job. I discussed it with Mavis and we agreed that we ought to seek further advice and so we booked an appointment with the local advice centre. The lady with whom we had the appointment read through the correspondence and told Mavis that from what she could see, we had very strong grounds for an appeal and referred us to another department

July 2007.

So much seemed to be happening all around us. It was our Ruby wedding anniversary this month and the girls and their families had clubbed together for us to have a weekend in the Lake District that was hot and wonderful. Also, Ailsa had just received news that, after over three years of jumping to every social workers whim, at last they had found a young lad of six who they were going to be allowed to adopt. All this excitement helped to distract Mavis from the benefits issue.

It would have been nice to have had some sort of formal recognition of 40 years of being married together, with all our friends and family, but I had to realise that we were broke. The building modifications had taken nearly all our savings and when a savings bond matured for £20,000, the bank took it, as it was the guarantee for the business when it failed because I was taking all my time looking after Mavis. If we didn't win the appeal we were going to be really up against it, as I would cease to be Mavis's carer and I would also have to try to find employment.

August 2007.

We had an appointment with the department that was going to handle our appeal. They agreed that they considered we had a very good case, so they registered all the papers and we awaited the information from the DWP to see how they were going to justify their case. When it arrived it consisted of 109 pages that all had to be gone through. It seemed that most of their case rested on the fact that they had written to the consultant at the hospital. His letter of reply had said that Mavis had walked into the consulting room unaided. This was in fact true and had been about six months earlier when Mavis had gone to see him as part of the usual follow up. I had been really proud of how well Mavis had done with her walking. She could now walk tentatively around the house without a stick. I was trying to encourage her and build up her confidence by persuading her to walk outside on her own as well. She had lost all confidence about walking outside in the street but I was hoping that in such places as hospitals, she might manage short distances. This had been one such occasion. She had walked from the waiting room into the consulting room about 10 yards by herself, which of course the Consultant had then seen as walking unaided! I pointed this out to the person handling the appeal and slowly our case was formed.

As a belt and braises job I went to see the consultant and we discussed Mavis's case in detail. It seems that after filling in the form that he was required to do, he also sent a letter to the DWP expanding on what he had written. He had felt that the form had asked certain questions but the answers given could not have reflected the true state of the situation. I have always said that in order to get the right answer you have to ask the right question and this time it seemed to be working against us. This seemed particularly true as only the form had been selected by the DWP to be used in evidence for the case, not the collateral letter.

Although Mavis had undoubtedly recovered more than anyone's wildest dreams could have imagined three years ago, her executive skills had still not returned. For example if she made a cup of coffee she could register that she had used the last of the milk, but she wouldn't be able to tell you how to go about getting more. You could sit with her and work it out, but the thought process would not carry over naturally. You could take Mavis to a busy shopping Mall and she would seem perfectly normal mentally but, if I had left her there on her own, apart from the physical impediment, I am sure that her brainpower would not have allowed her to find her own way home. Another example was that she could feel thirsty, but would always ask me to make a drink for her, even though she was capable of making it herself and she was never a lazy person.

October 23rd 2007.

The day of the appeal. It was a nice sunny day and at any other time we would have been able to enjoy it to the full. We met our representative and together we went into the courtroom. The Panel consisted of a solicitor, a doctor and a disabled person/carer and one by one, they asked Mavis many questions. After the first question, Mavis started to cry and so I had to explain that this was not because they were asking her questions but that it was a result of the way her stroke had left her. We had nothing to hide and all the questions were answered honestly. One particular question brought about a lighter side to the proceedings when the solicitor asked Mavis again how far she could walk and how long it took her. Mavis answered that if she was walking along to our neighbours, which was about 25 yards, it usually took her about 15 minutes on her own and she could only do that if the weather conditions were very good i.e. not windy or slippery. The Doctor then asked if she was very tired by the time she walked back. "Not really" replied Mavis "I always stop for a cup of coffee and have a rest."

We were asked to leave the room while the panel did their deliberations. We had hardly sat down when we were asked to return. To our great relief the panel had found in our favour. They agreed with us that Mavis could not look after herself on her own and she needed a great deal of help with mobility, personal hygiene, and sustenance.

They commended Mavis on her dogged determination, established exactly what benefits Mavis could retain and wished us well. We left a very relieved couple. As a comment though, it struck me that this was again a terrible waste of resource and money. If only someone had gone to see Mavis and talked to her, they could have seen both her physical and emotional state and all this could have been avoided.

And so we come to the end of a chapter of our lives that although not wanting or expecting has blessed us both richly.

It has proved to us that the medics can be wrong and thank goodness for that.

It has brought Mavis and I very close together. When the children were about and Helen was with us, we said that something we were both looking forward to was spending some quality time together. As they say, be careful what you pray for. God may answer your prayers, but not always in the way you expect it to happen.

It has also shown us that God is sovereign. Through working in and through Mavis, he has shown us his love and care for both her and me. That really is something so wonderful that we can't understand why everyone cannot believe he exists.

Mavis continues to make slow but steady progress. I continue to encourage her where I can and we have now taken holidays that even we thought would not have been possible a few years ago. We continue to work on her left hand and she is now able to move her fingers individually to order although nothing has returned to the shoulder yet. Whether she will be able to return to reasonable functionality only the Lord knows but Mavis borrowed some music from our daughters and I resurrected an old key board that has lain dormant on top of a wardrobe for the last umteen years. This year Mavis wants to be able to play the piano again. Who knows?

Mavis's input cont./

All through these last five years, it has only been the constant love of Mike, Heather, and Ailsa that has enabled me to want to continue the fight to recover as much as it is possible. On many occasion it would have been so easy to give up, but their constant encouragement has made it all very much worthwhile. I have much to thank the Lord for. Every morning I wake up thinking "what am I going to do today" and it is so exciting.

Help Points.

In Hospital.

Make sure YOU know what is going on. Ask questions and if unsure query and ask again.

Monitor the patient yourself. After all, you probably know them better than anyone else does

Monitor the observation charts (usually at the bottom of the bed). Don't rely on the nurses to keep you informed they may be too busy.

If YOU think things are not happening or going as they should, talk to the ward sister and if nothing improves take it higher. It is an unfortunate fact that those people who shout the most usually get the most done.

Be aware! Is the patient able to reach their liquids and able to eat their food themselves. If not, are they being helped or simply left to their own devices.

A high percentage of adults normally carry MRSA around with them in normal life. Protect your patient (and the others in the ward) by always washing with the gel both going in and out of the ward.

Use your time at the hospital in every way you can to help you and the patient come to terms with what has happened and plan for the fullest recovery possible. No one knows what that will be although you will come across several theories.

Out of Hospital.

Be Prepared! Will your patient need a RADAR key? (Disabled persons toilet key) If so, contact your council they will tell you how to obtain one.

The same applies with the Blue Badge for transport. Even if you don't have a car you will find it a lot easier if you qualify, whenever someone else takes the patient to the hospital/shopping.

Are you claiming all the benefits you will need to help you survive? Obtain the forms and ask an expert to help you fill them in. Most councils run schemes to help those who need to fill in benefits forms properly. It can make a huge difference.

If the patient used to drive, have you informed the DVLA of the change in their circumstances? It is against the law not to do so.

Do you need modifications to your house_to make day-to-day living easier? The Hospital Occupational Therapist will help. If major building modifications are required, then grants are available.

Will the patient need an electric wheelchair? If so, find out what the qualifying criteria are as it varies enormously from council to council. Also, find out what the waiting period is, as you may need to provide your own in the short term.

Does the patient need an ordinary or transfer wheelchair. If so, ask if you can contribute yourself to having a better, lighter chair or if the council run a voucher scheme. This is where they give you a voucher to the amount they would pay for a chair. You can then take this to a provider, choose a chair of choice and just pay the difference if there is any.

Above all encourage/ push/ shove/ offer carrots and if necessary use sticks to get the patient to make as complete a recovery as possible. It's not only their life that has been affected. Yours and the rest of the family has been too. Nearly every stroke survivor I have met has lost so much of the self-confidence that they had pre stroke. It will be very hard work to rebuild it, but ultimately it has to be worth it, as making their life easier will also make yours better too.

Appendix 1

Copy of letter sent to the ward to complain

Catalogue of Errors concerning Mrs. Mavis Brewster
D.O.B. 03.10.43

15/06/04   A & E dept ECG monitor connected incorrectly Doctor forced to investigate and rectify.

16/06/04   Urine bag emptied on medical ward and not resealed therefore Urine deposited all over floor when moved to ASW D41.

21/06/04   Patient complaining of pain at top of legs. I investigate to find sores between top of leg and body. Point this out to nurse to uses Sudacream? to rectify. Surely if the body was being properly attended to these sores should not have arisen in the first place.

22/06/04   Patient able to start feeding herself for first time. Given filthy cutlery to eat with. I notice although fluids to be encouraged, table with fluids on always left at bottom of bed out of reach.

24/06/04   Meet Physiotherapist who advises patient too tired to start active physio but says paralysed arm should be supported at all times with a pillow to save shoulder. I notice that on every occasion visited, no pillow for support.

26/06/04   I notice many meals refused. Asked patient why but too fatigued to answer. Therefore, I assume too fatigued to feed herself.

27/06/04   Nurse comes to take blood sugar levels, pricks finger on good hand without cleaning it and says she has to inform doctor that sugar level in 13. I suggest she takes it again after cleaning finger as patient just finished sipping juice from cup. Sugar level determined now to be 8.7. Even more disconcerting is to find slightly moist tablets on patient's chest. Conclude these have dropped out from paralysed side of mouth, patient being unaware. Surely, staff have a responsibility to ensure patients are able to take their medication!

27/06/04   14:00 We notice from notes there is no mention of Bowel movements. Ask Nurse to investigate. Agrees no bowel movement since admittance so 13 days of constipation. Suggest something be done and told this is common in stroke patients and therefore the doctor would not do anything for at least another two days. 18:00 Nurse now says can have treatment and pill will be given at 22:00. At 20:00 pill given. Nurse asks us to tell her what fluids have been consumed as nobody had recorded it.

28/06/04   Physio arrives to do initial assessment. Patient lifted into chair and left in care of nurses to wash patient. Urine bag left on floor for people to tread on so I pick up and put in bowl to protect both bag and catheterised patient. Still notice arm never supported when visiting.

29/06/04   Patient put in chair at 10:00 and left until I asked for her to be returned to bed at 20:15 as she is very uncomfortable and that left arm was dangling down over side of chair and had been for some considerable time from the way the skin had stuck to vinyl. Arm was very cold and slightly swollen Shouted at by Nurse that they had other patients to attend to. 21:00. Two nurses arrive to put patient back to bed. Told I must leave and very aggressively told that Patient had been asked twice during the day if she had wished to be returned to bed but had refused. This being unacceptable I complained to senior on night duty a) about lack of nursing skills, b) about lack of care and c) about Nurse's attitude. Spoke to Dr. about concerns over constipation and he agreed to raise level of laxative.

01/07/04   Arrived as usual at 08:30 to ensure patient gets fed. I notice Urine bag empty assume it's just been emptied. Stayed until

11:00. Return 13:00 for same reason and again noticed Urine bag empty. Left 14:30. Returned 16:30 to note Urine bag still empty and report to Nurse. Nurse examines and discovers catheter has been blocked and no urine output recorded. Patient has now been unable to pass urine for at least 8 hours while all the time I am trying my very best to encourage her to take fluids! Meantime the evening meal is served and once again, the cutlery has to be returned, as it is unclean. I ask the Nurse about why the urine had not been monitored and she accepted that it should have been but they were too busy. I also noted to the Nurse that to my knowledge the patient was still constipated. She checked, agreed, and said she would write it in the Doctors book. I was also informed that the skin on the patient's buttocks is beginning to break down and that they have removed the catheter.

And this is only day 16.